"Wow! Thank you for getting 'Enchanted Animal Kingdom'! Your awesome choice means a lot! Get ready for a wild adventure as you color your way through this magical book. Let your imagination run wild and have a blast bringing these cool animals to life! Thanks for joining the fun! Happy coloring! From, R&J Shop Global"

RJ&J Shop Global

2024

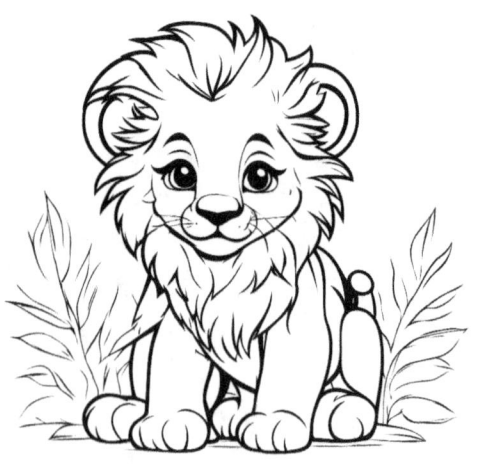
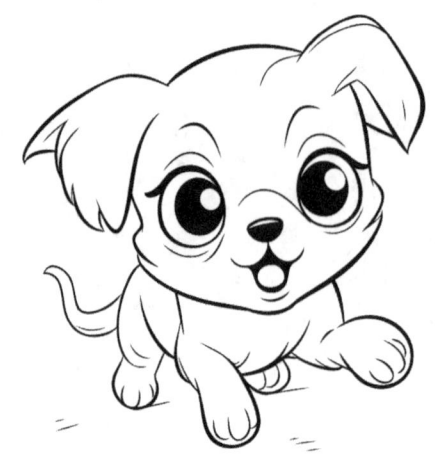

This Book Belongs to:

_____

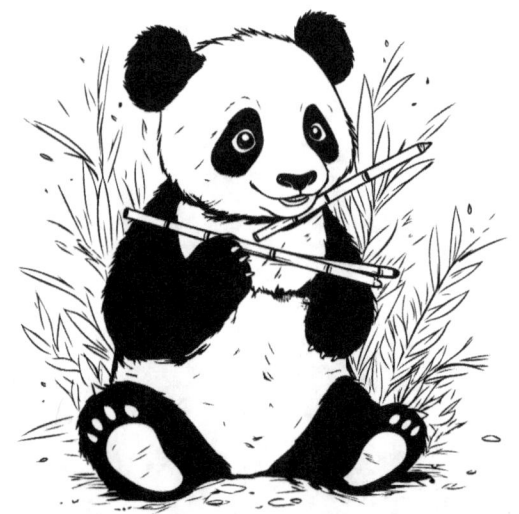
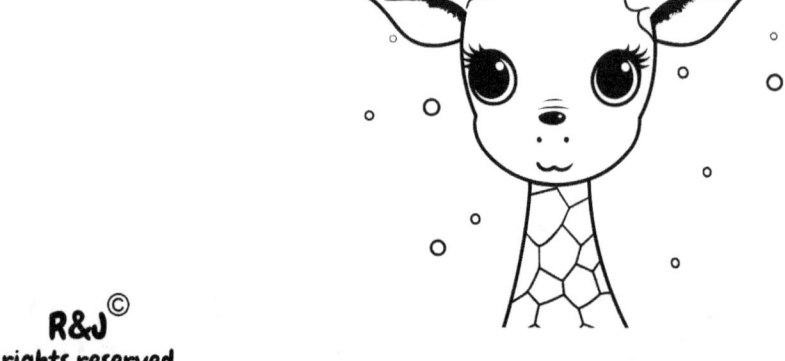

ALL RIGHTS RESERVED ©
2023

No part of this publication may be reproduced, distributed, or transmitted in any form or by any means, including photocopying, recording, or other electronic or mechanical methods, without the prior written permission of the publisher, except for brief quotations incorporated in critical reviews and other specific noncommercial uses. Any unauthorized replica of this work is prohibited.

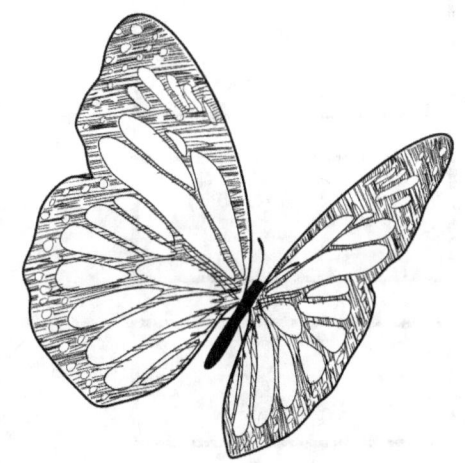

R&J©
Shop Global Shop Global

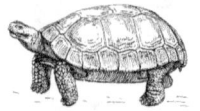 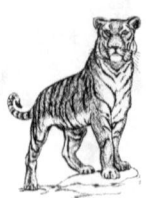

Test Color Page

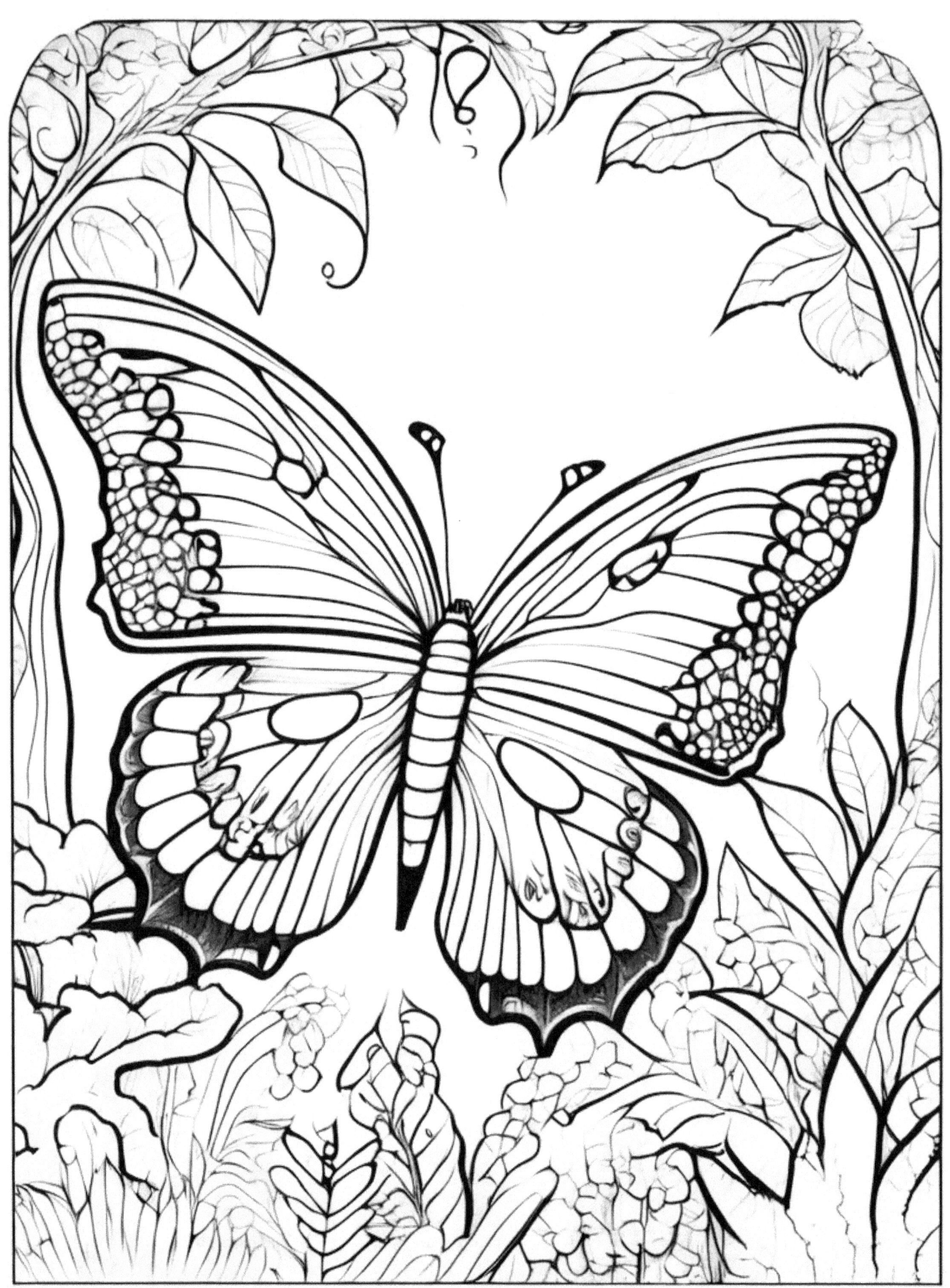

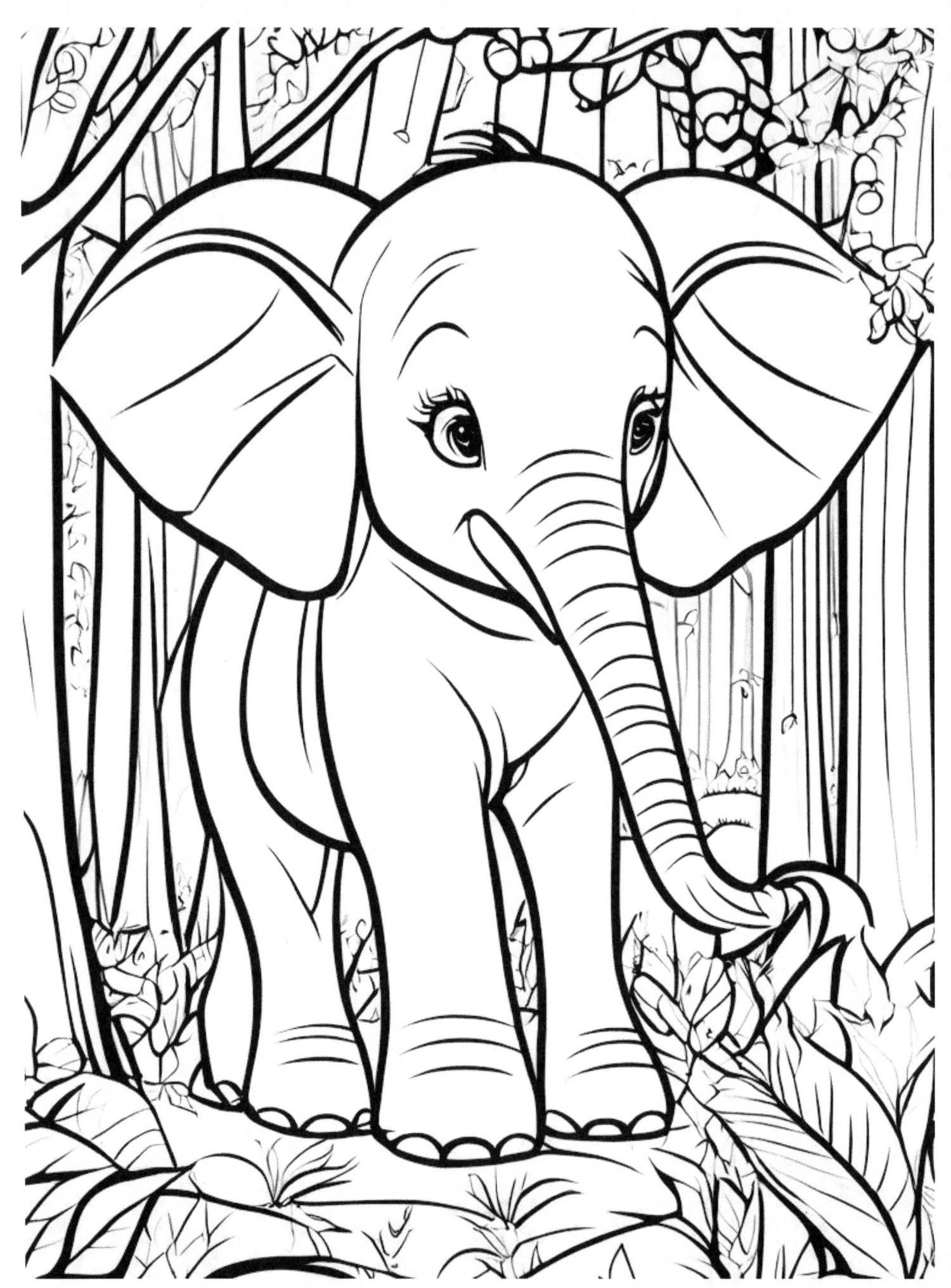

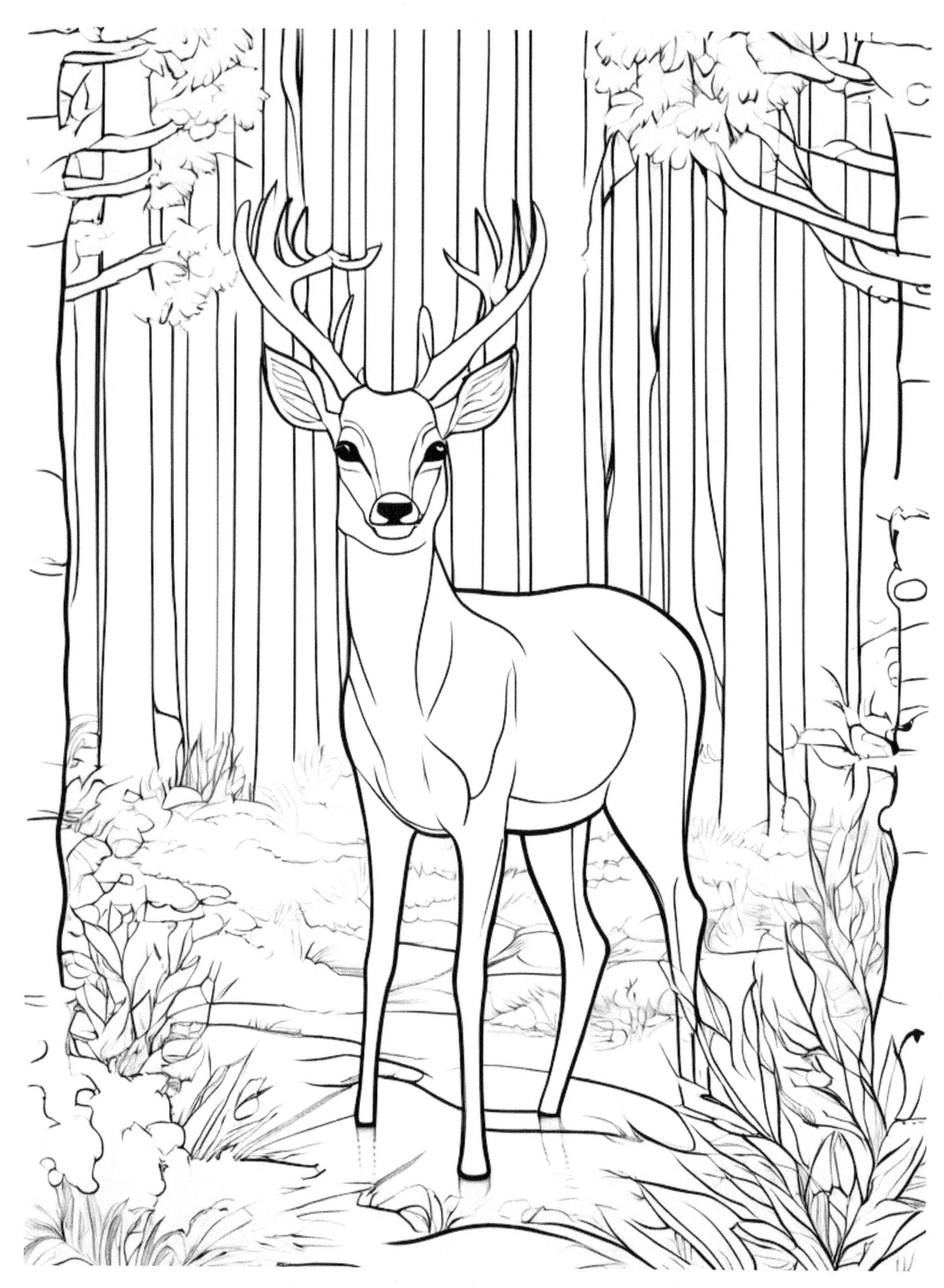

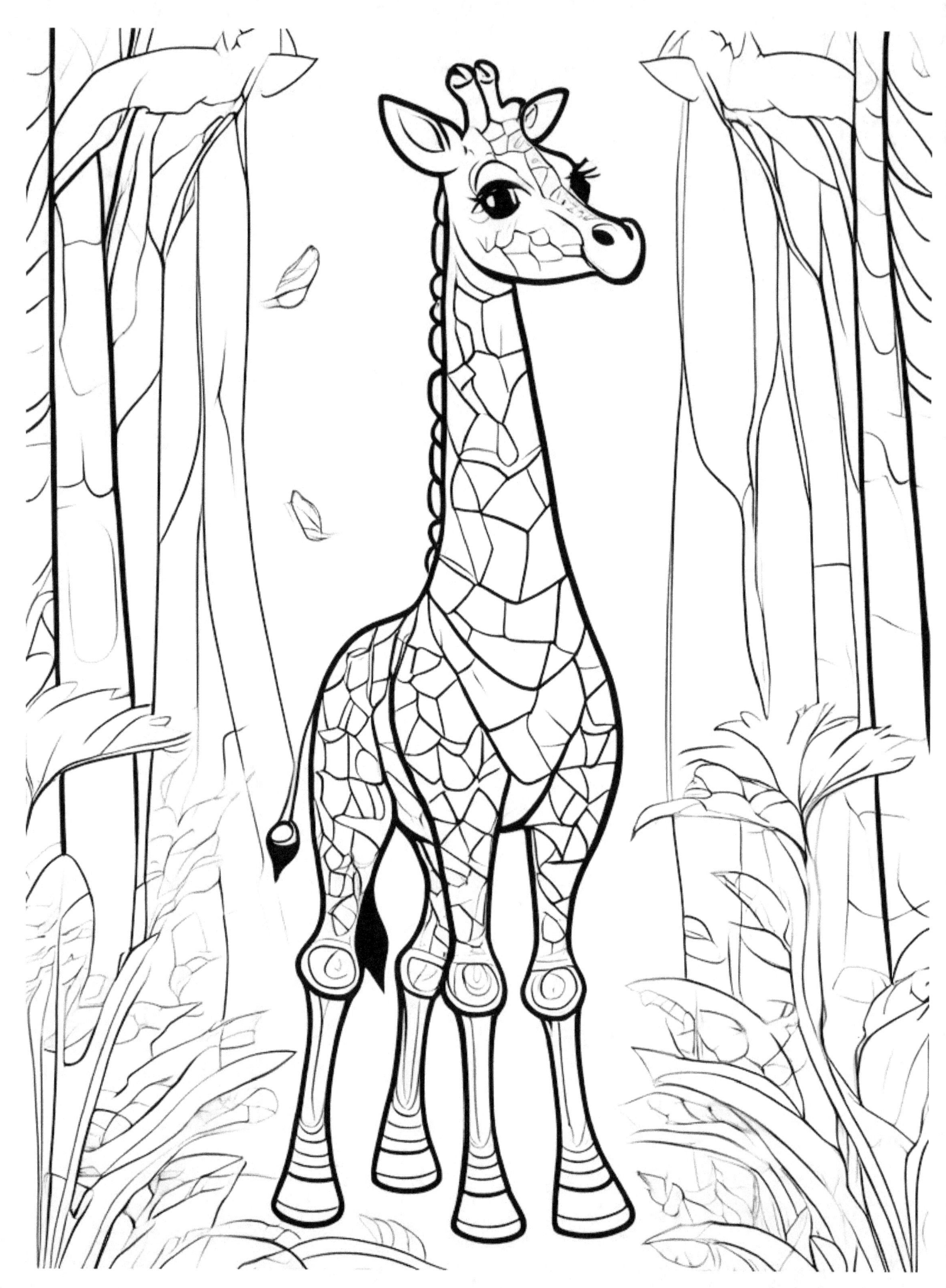

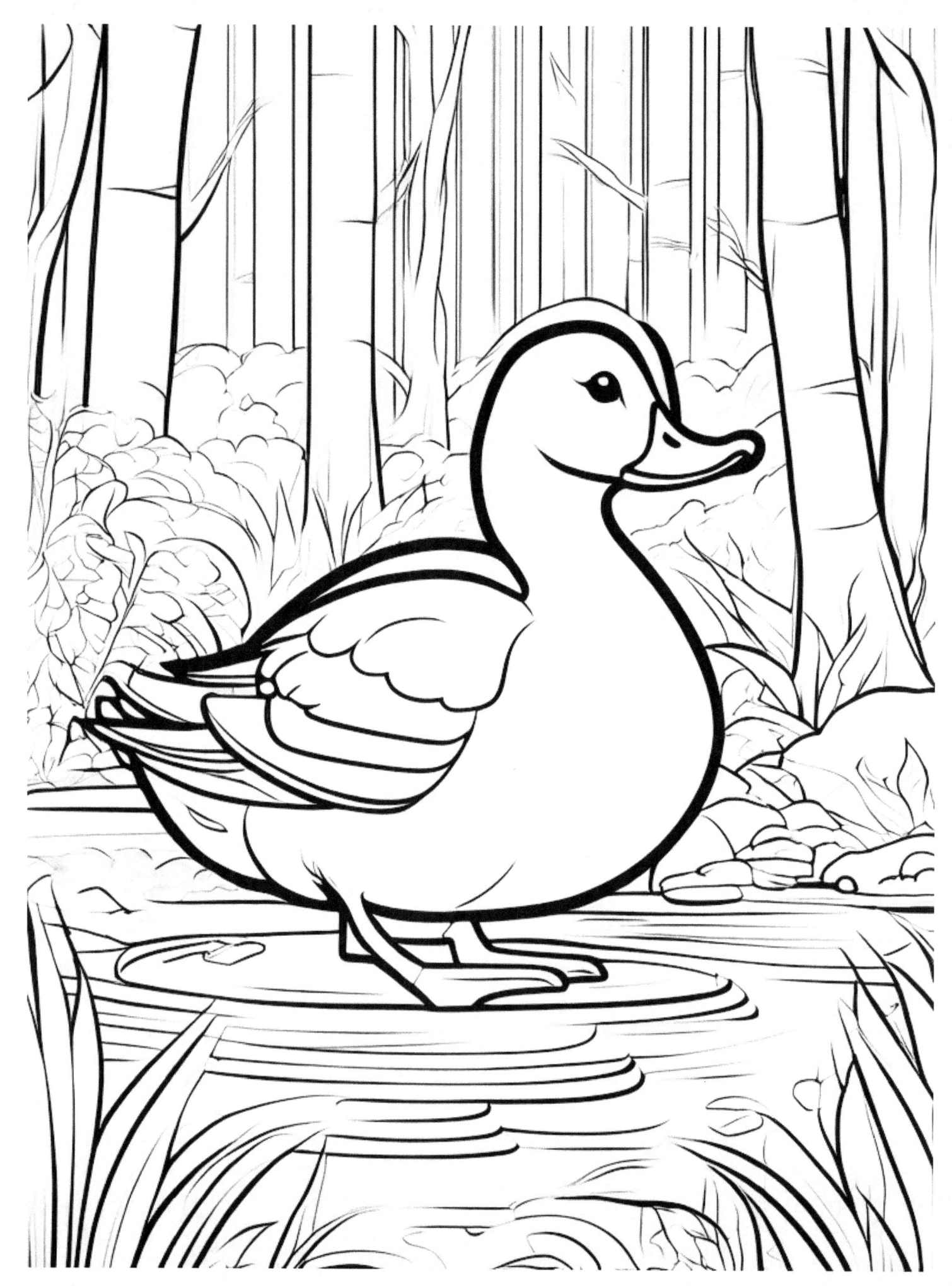

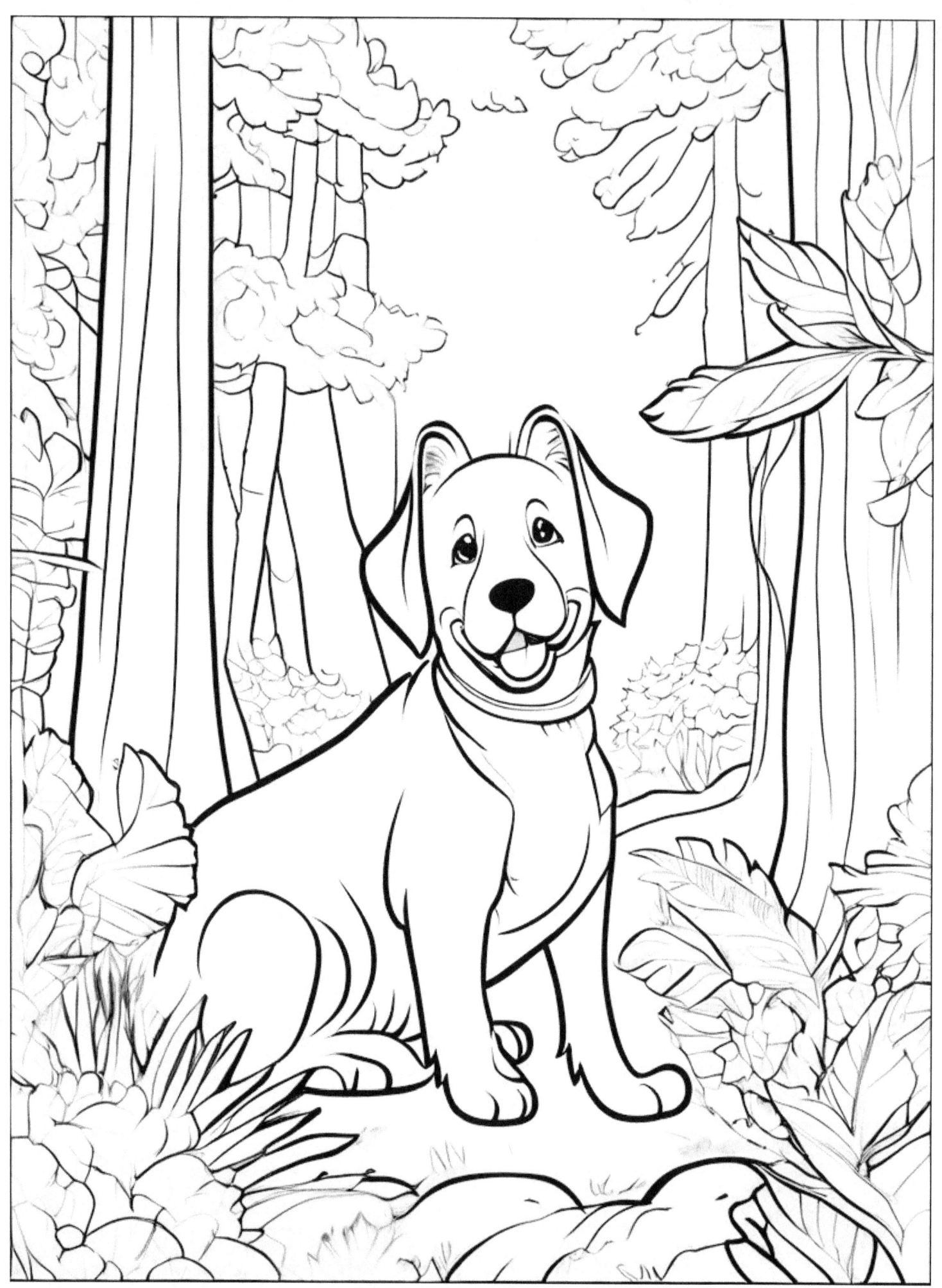

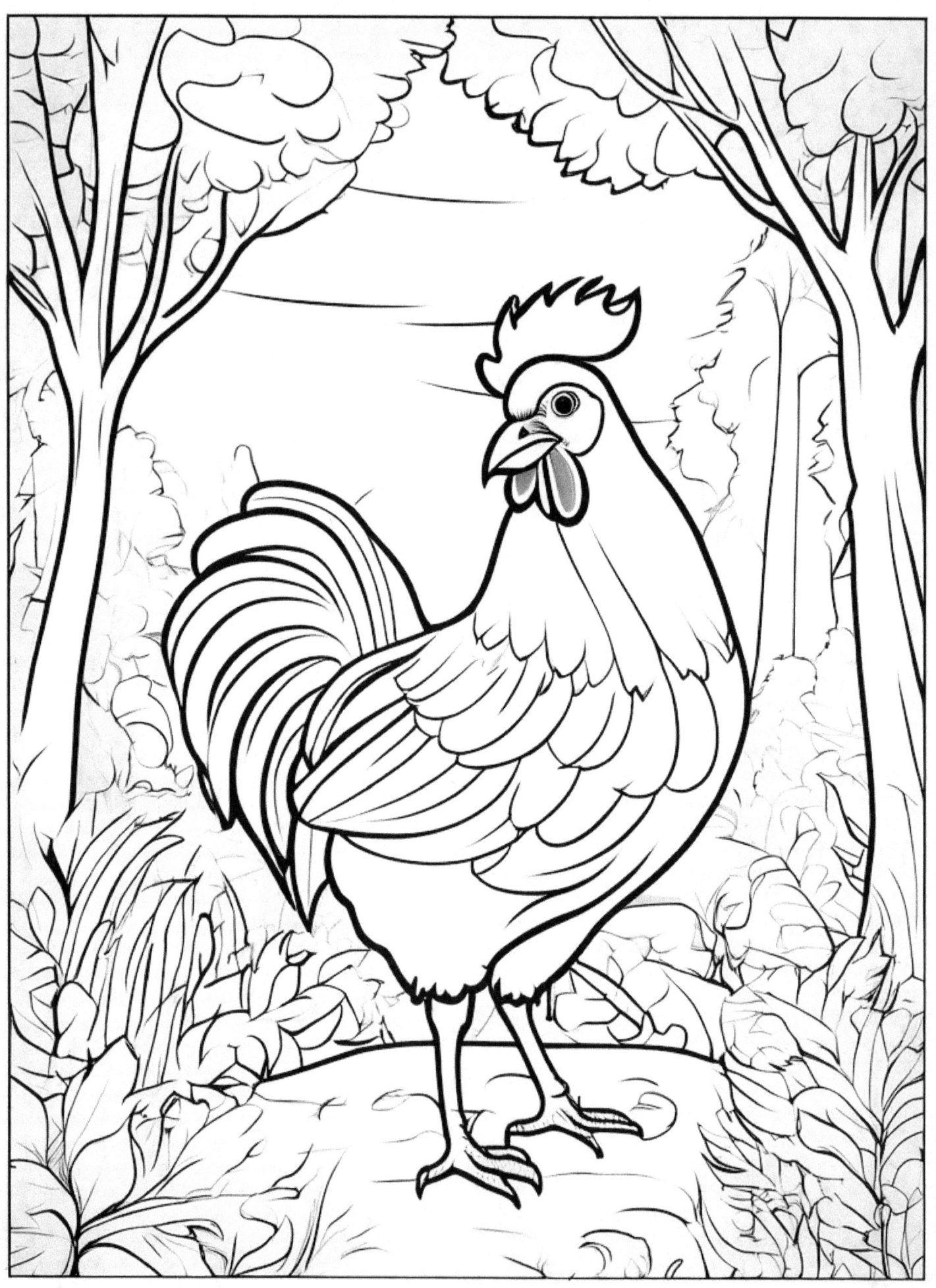

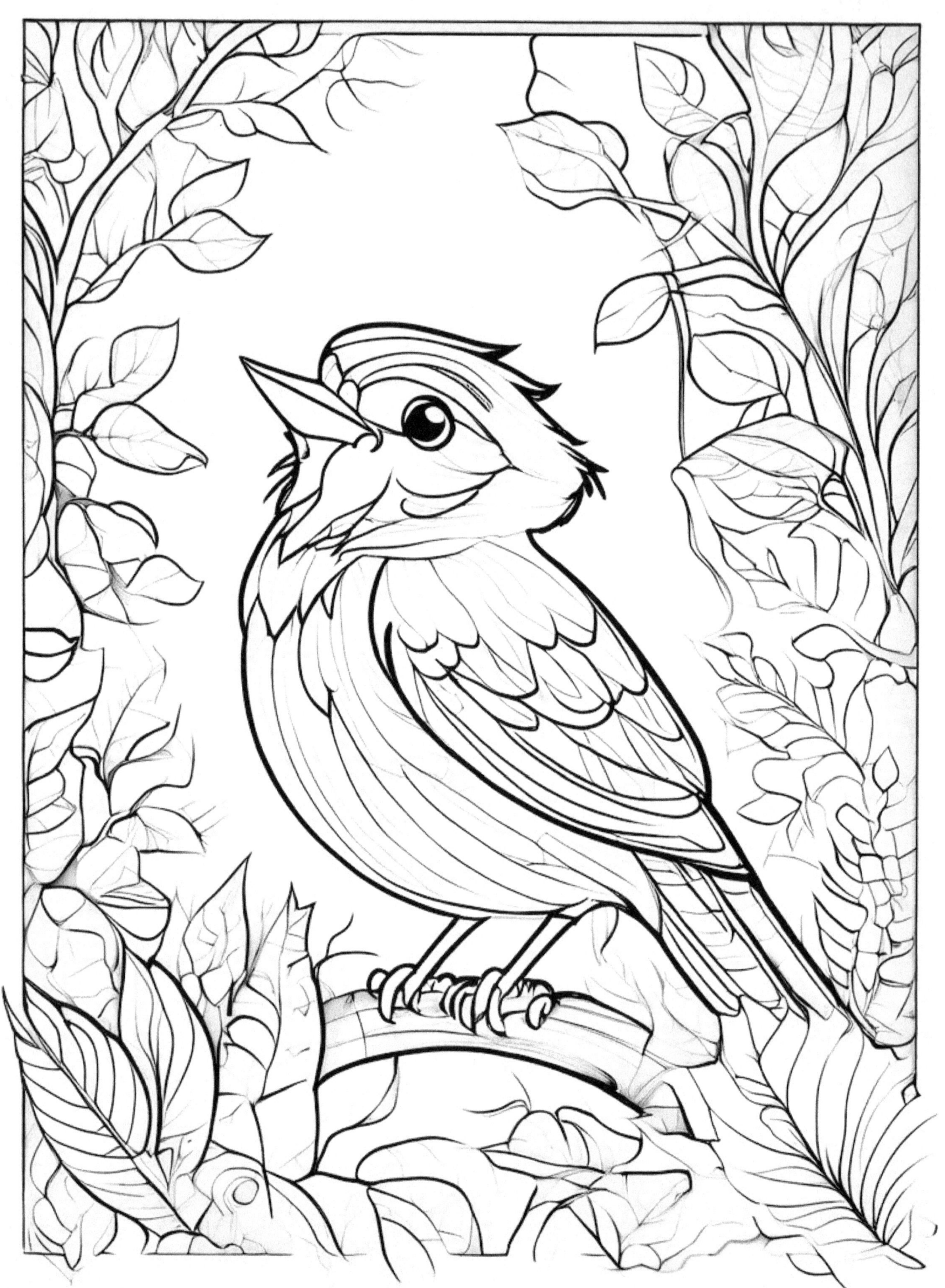

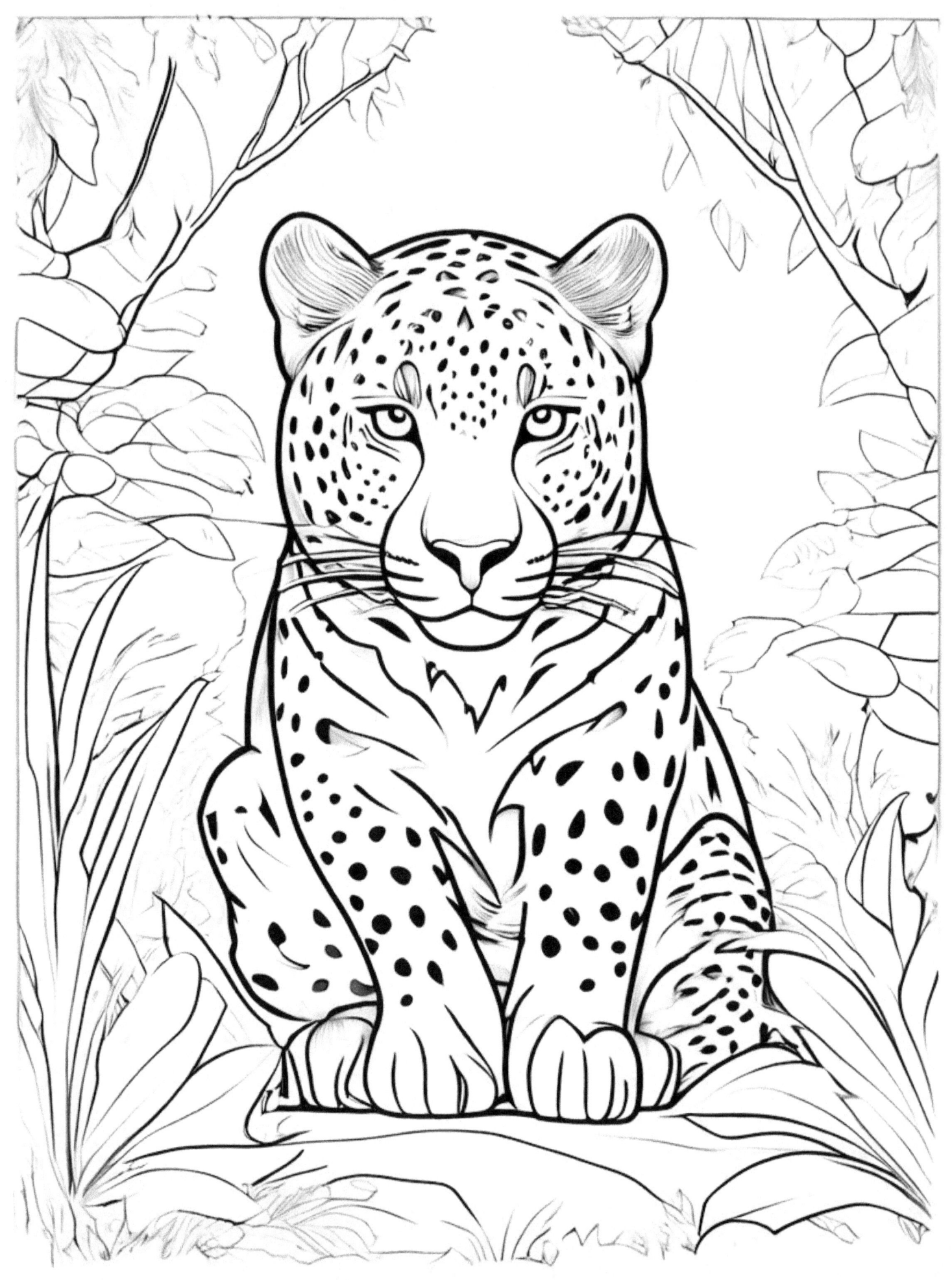

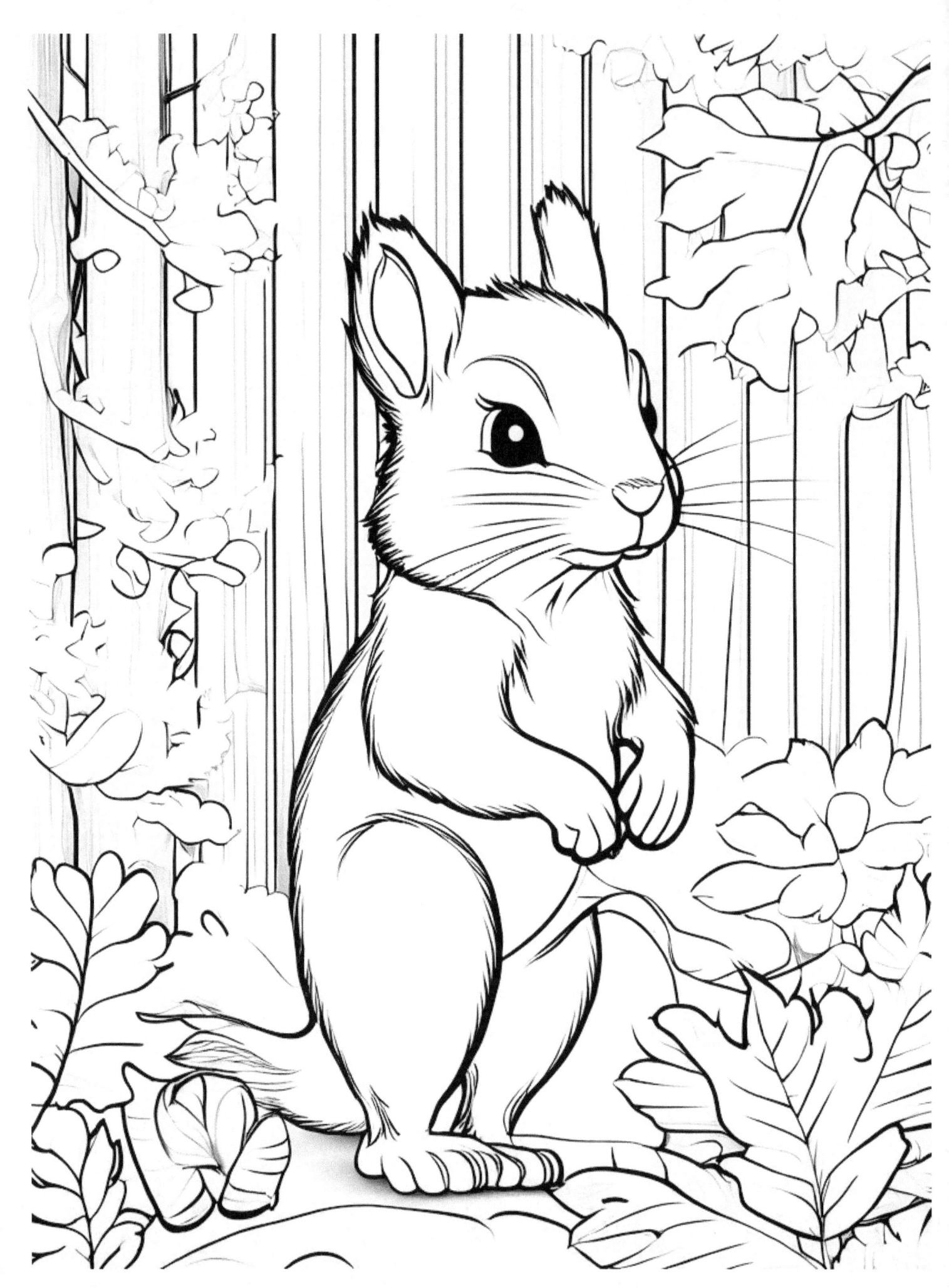

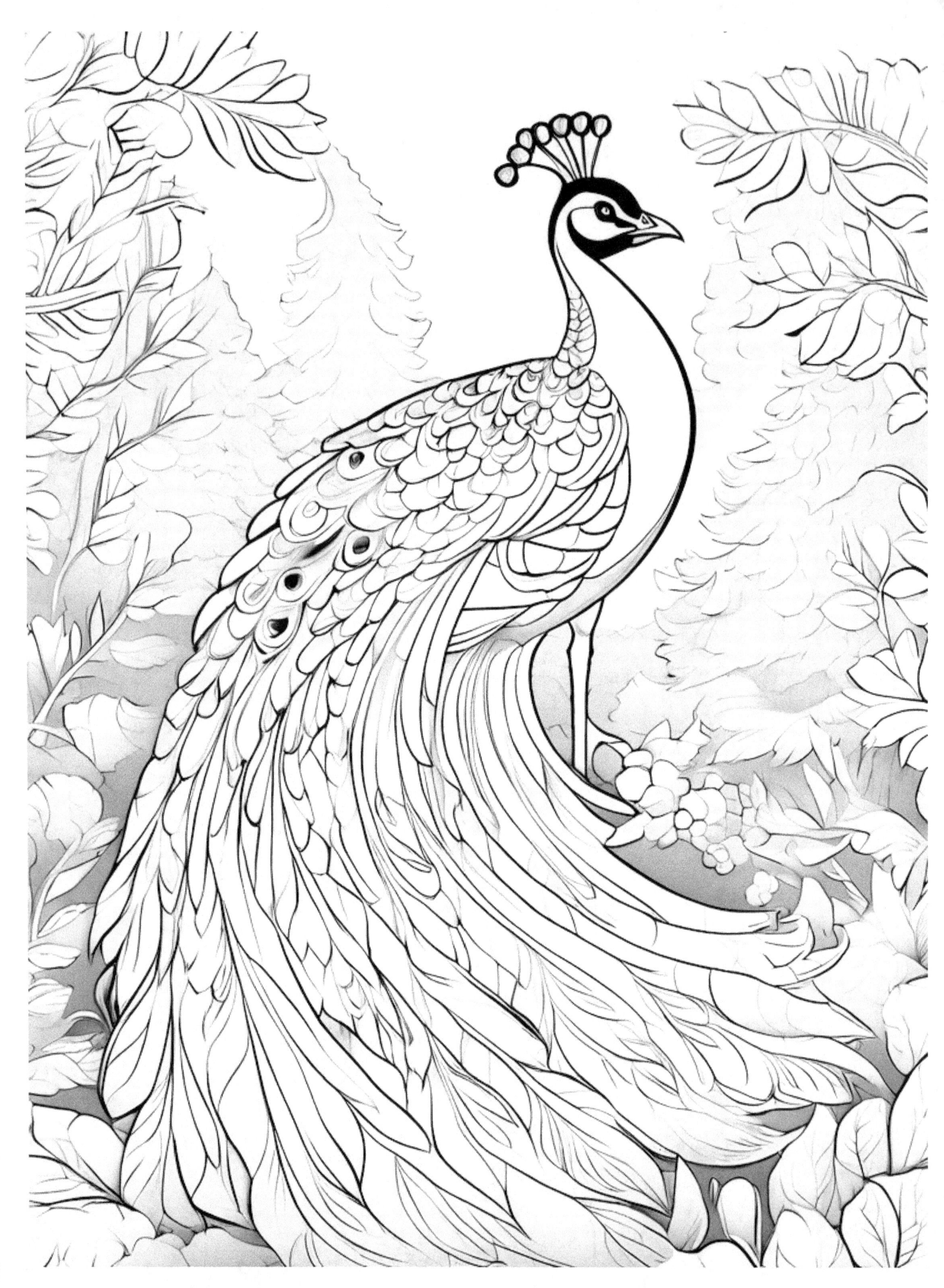

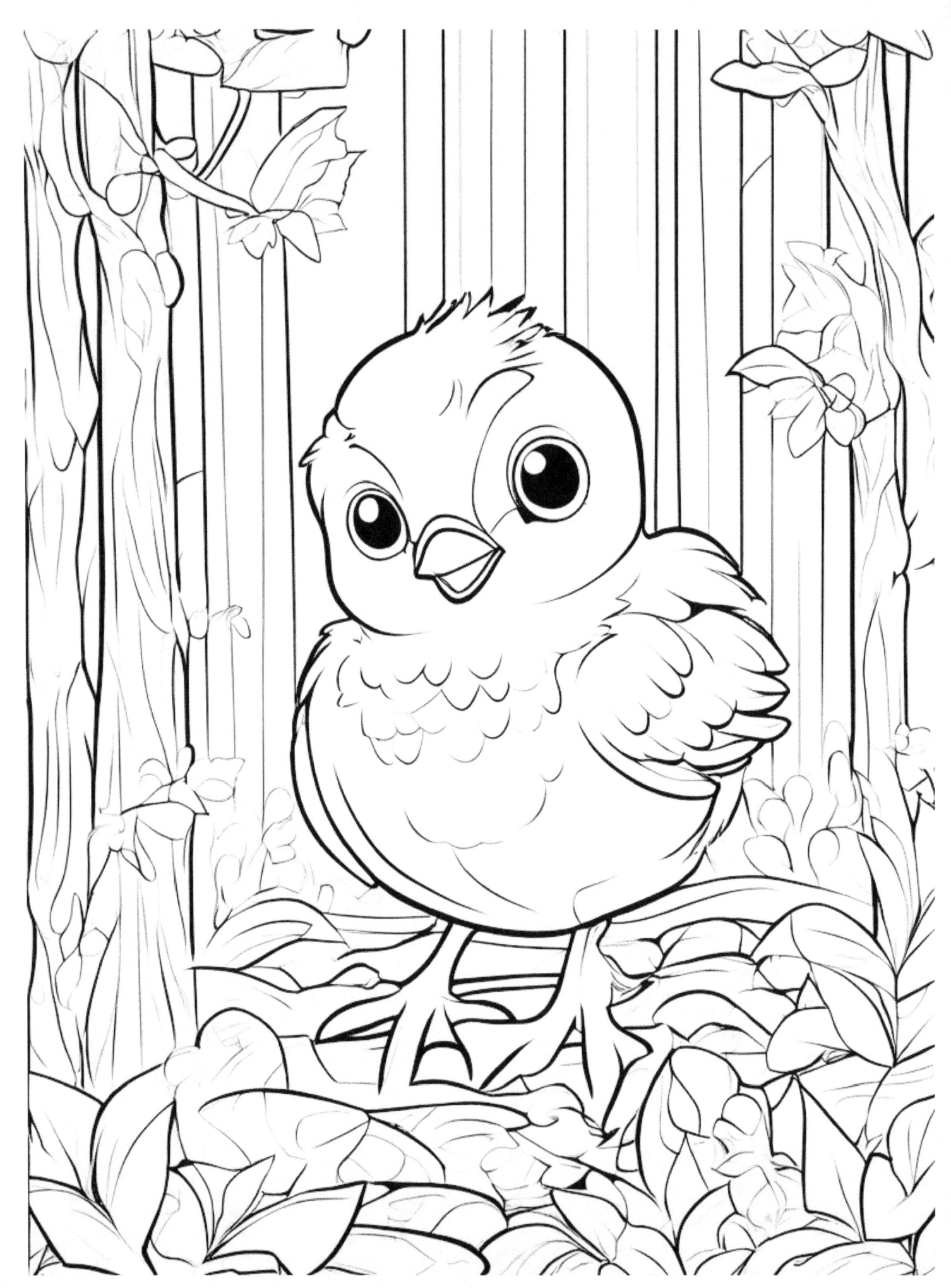

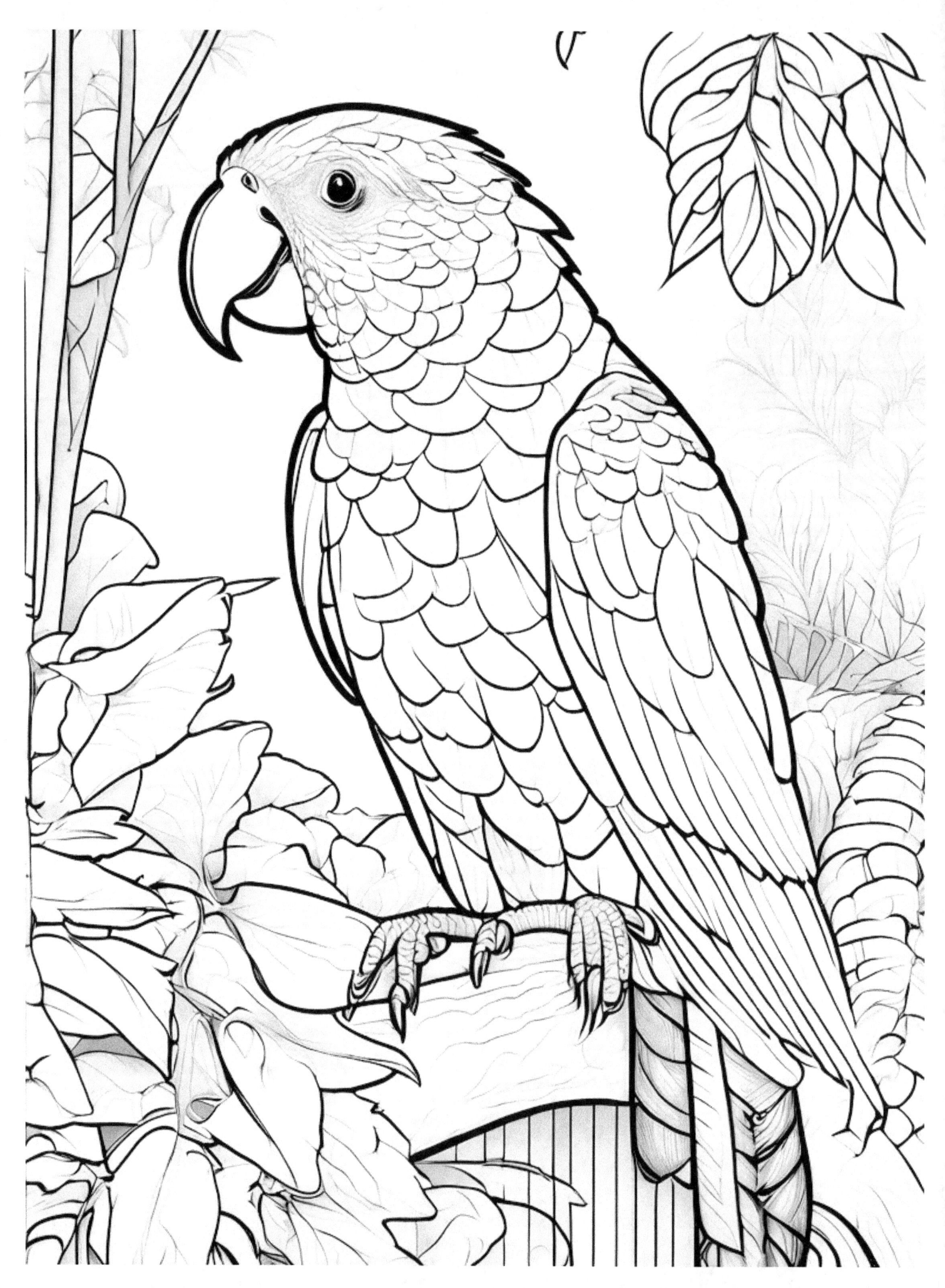

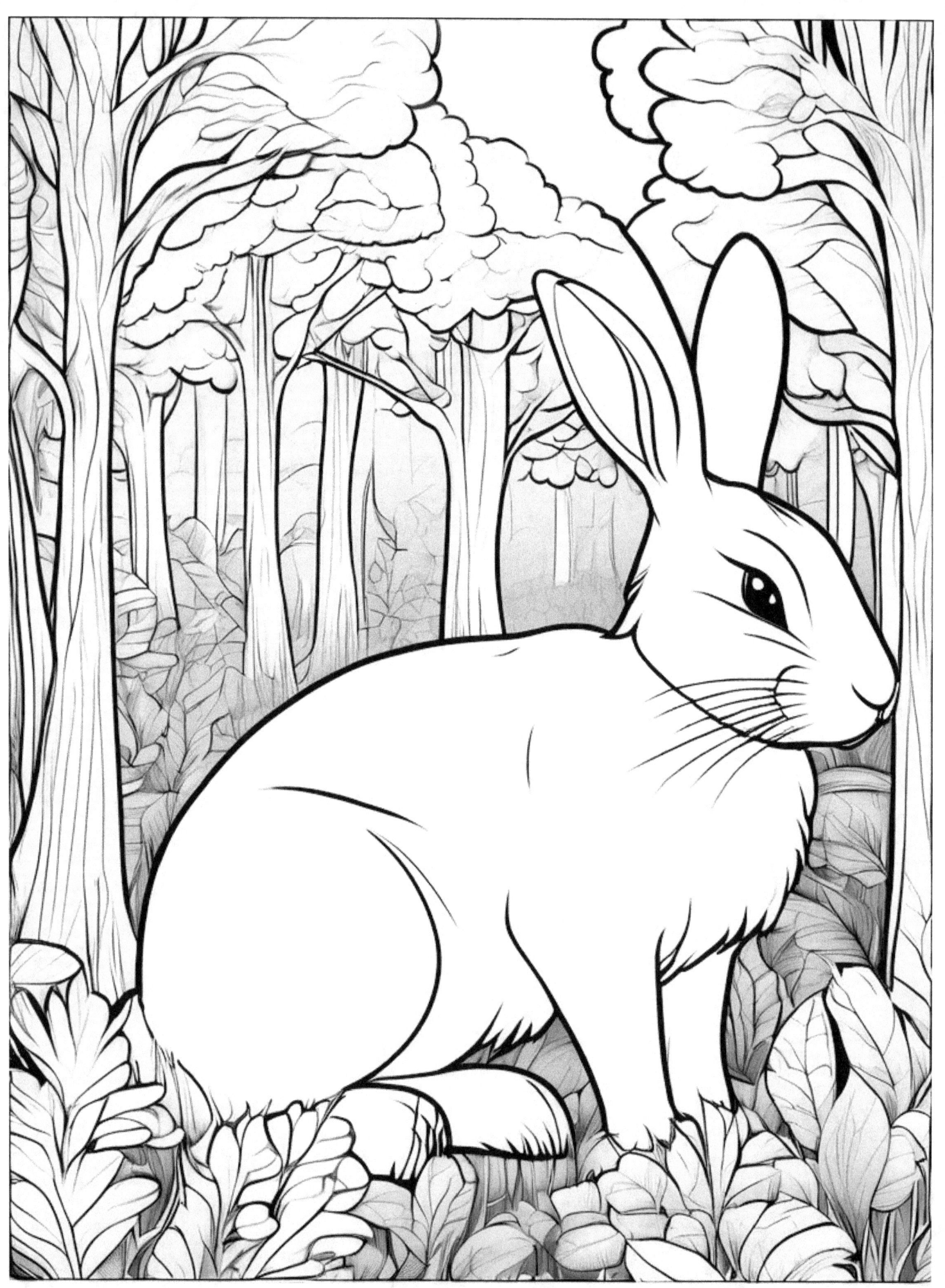

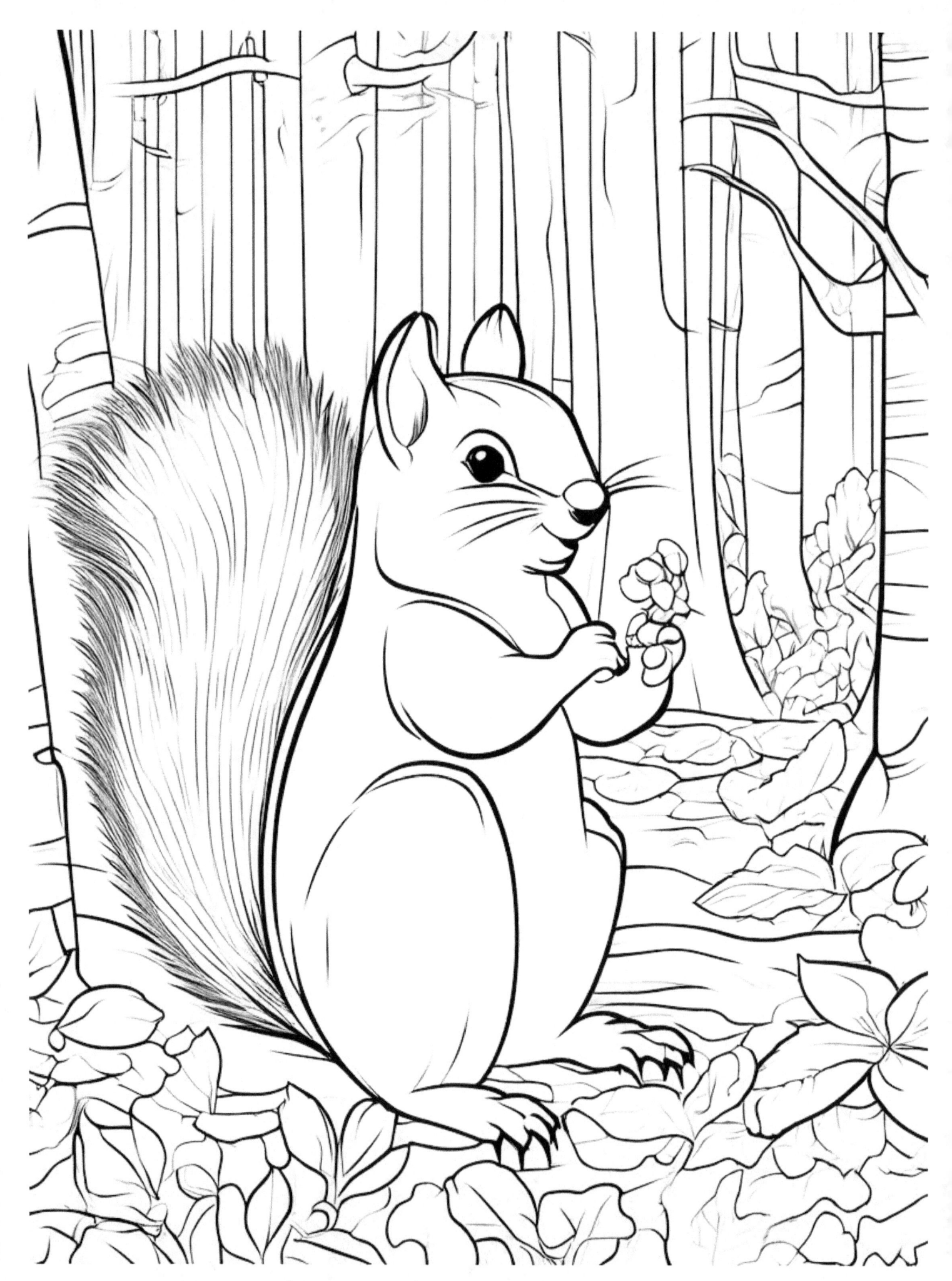

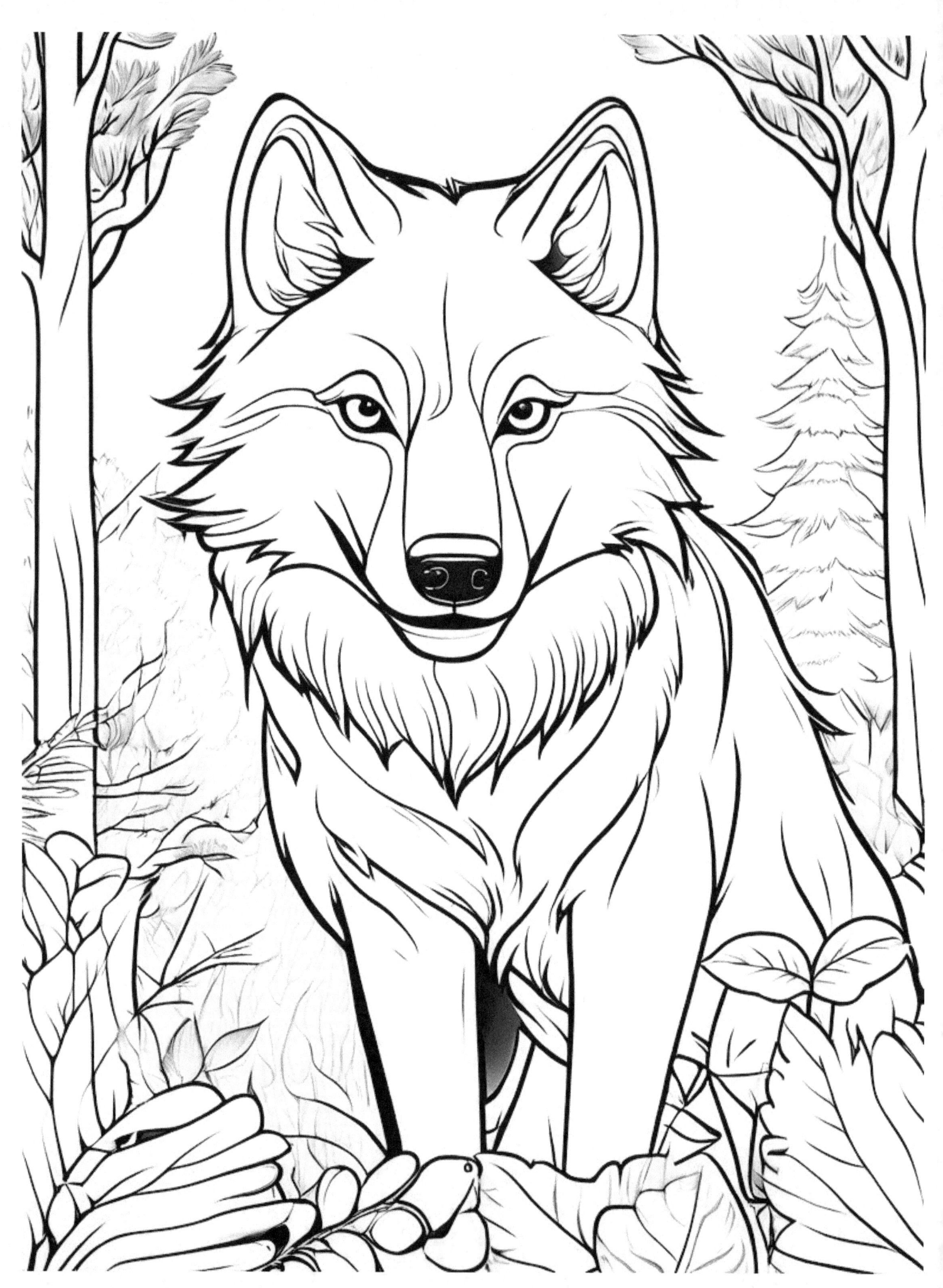

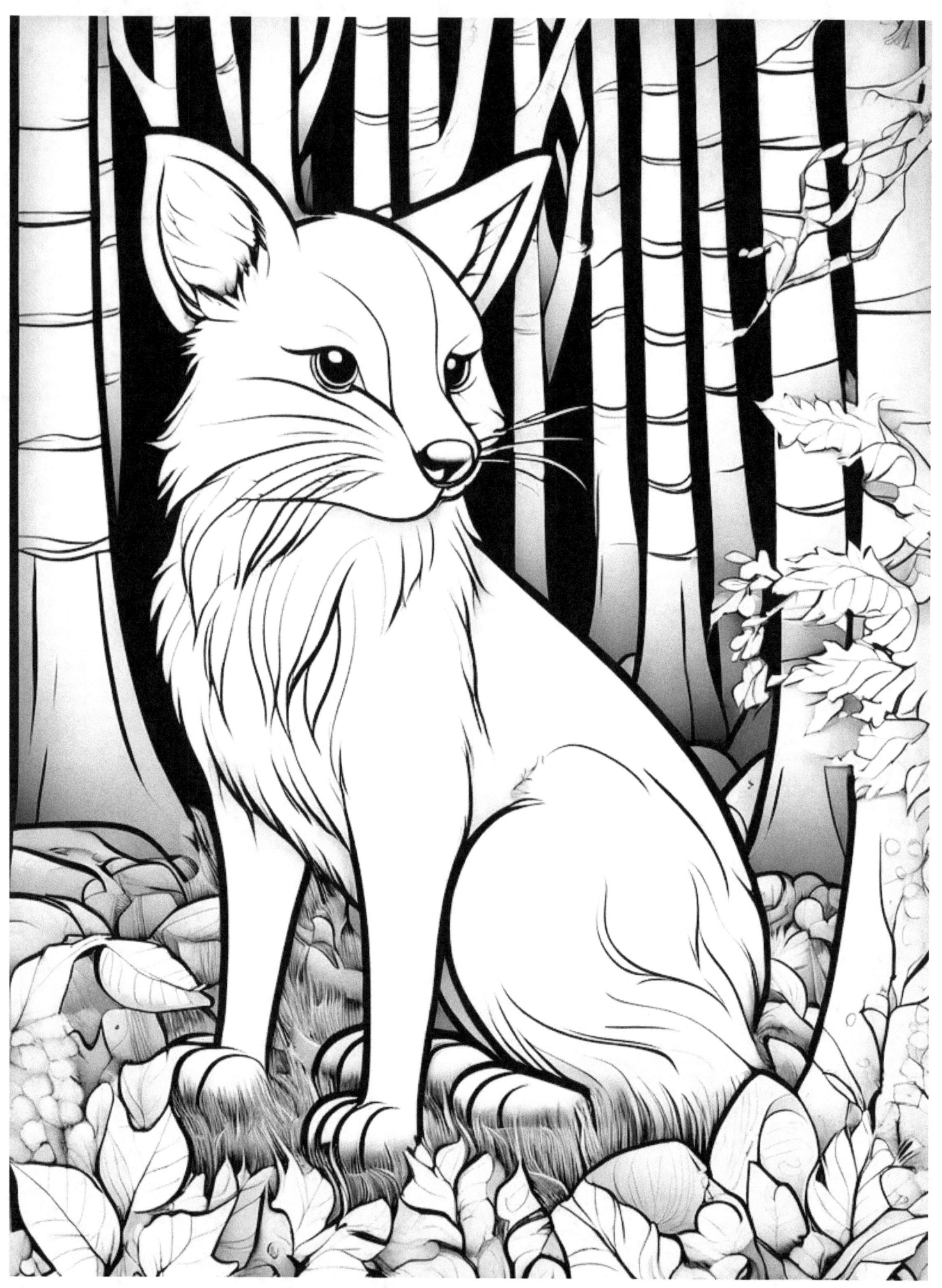

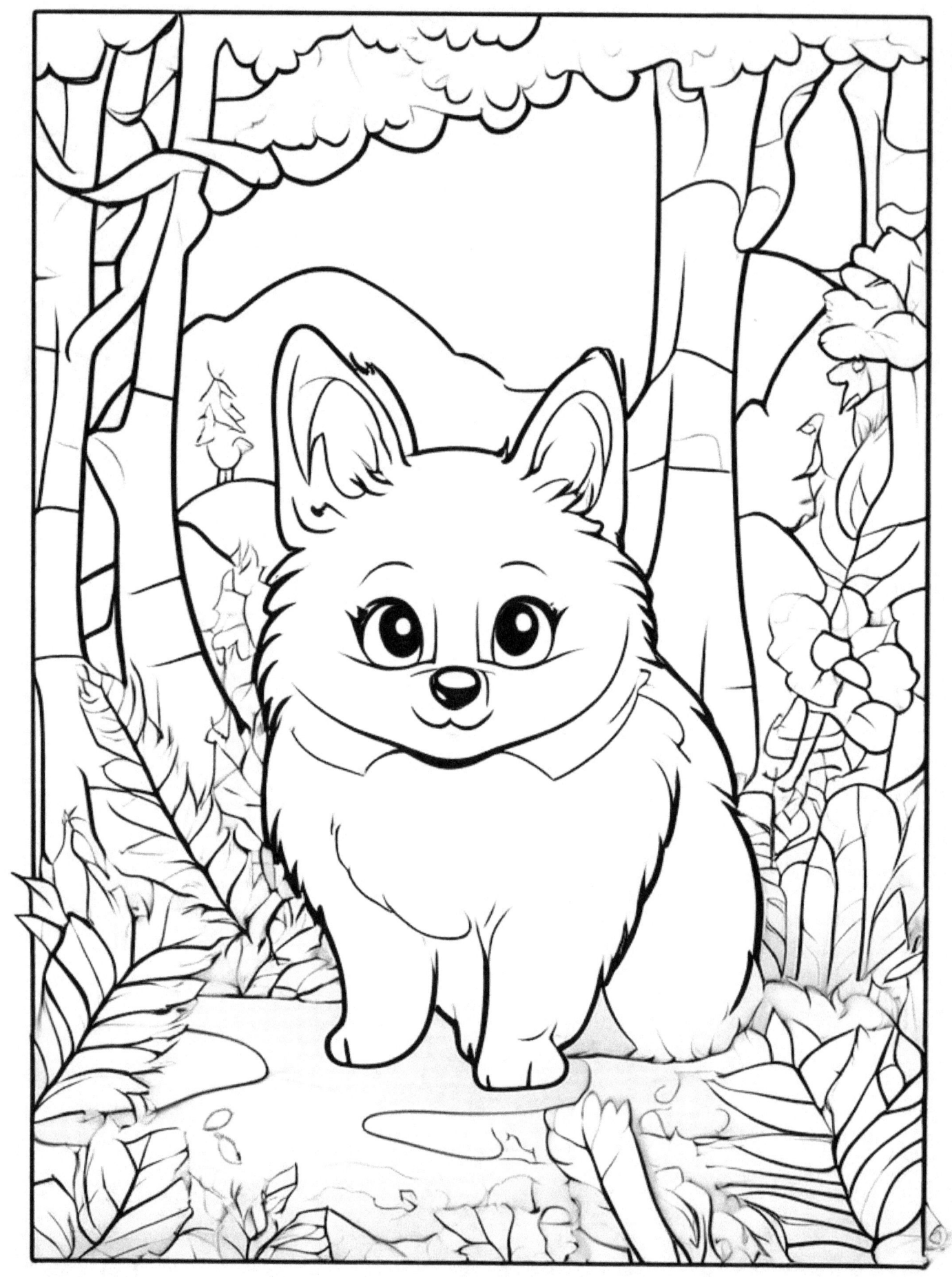

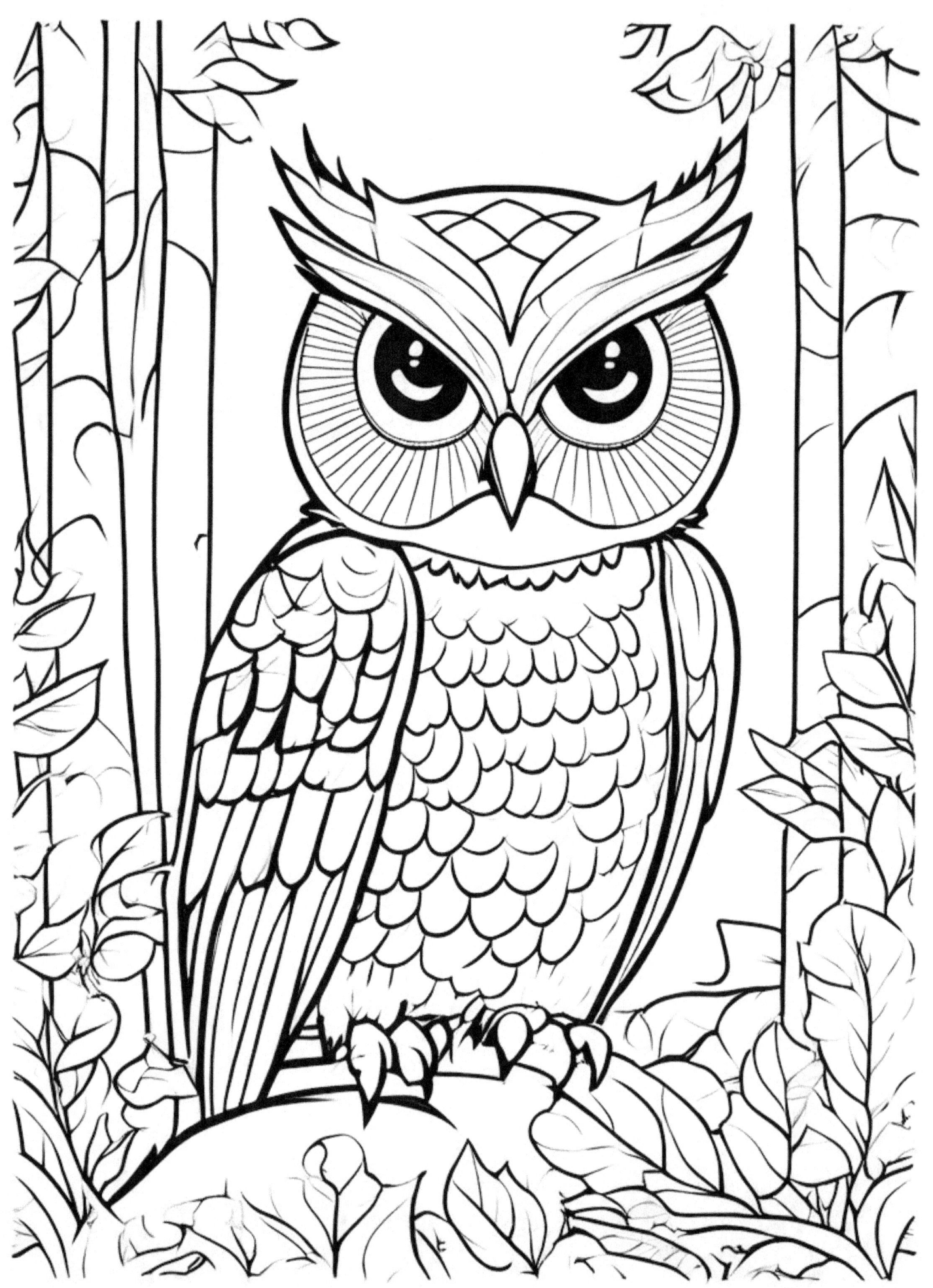

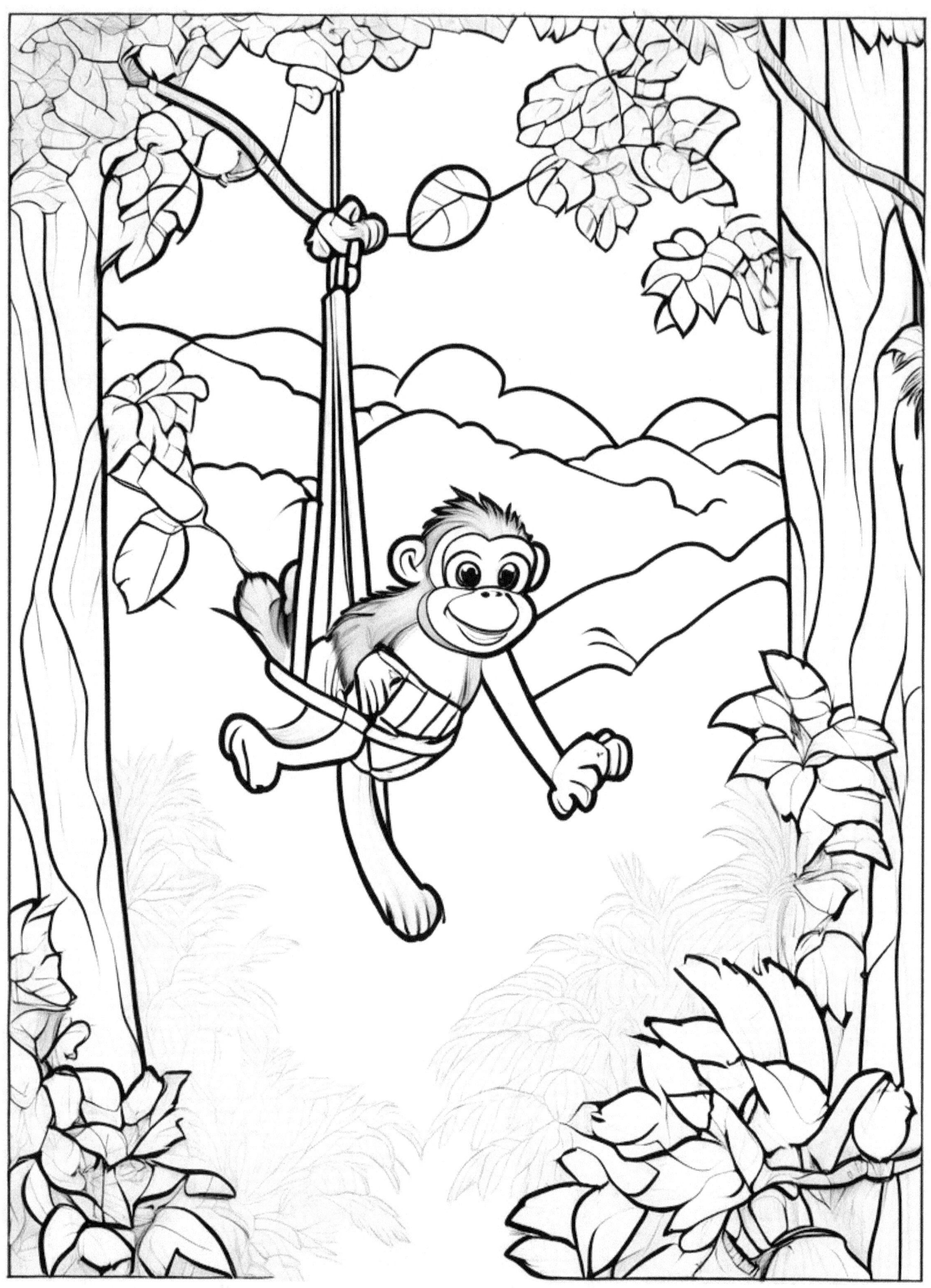

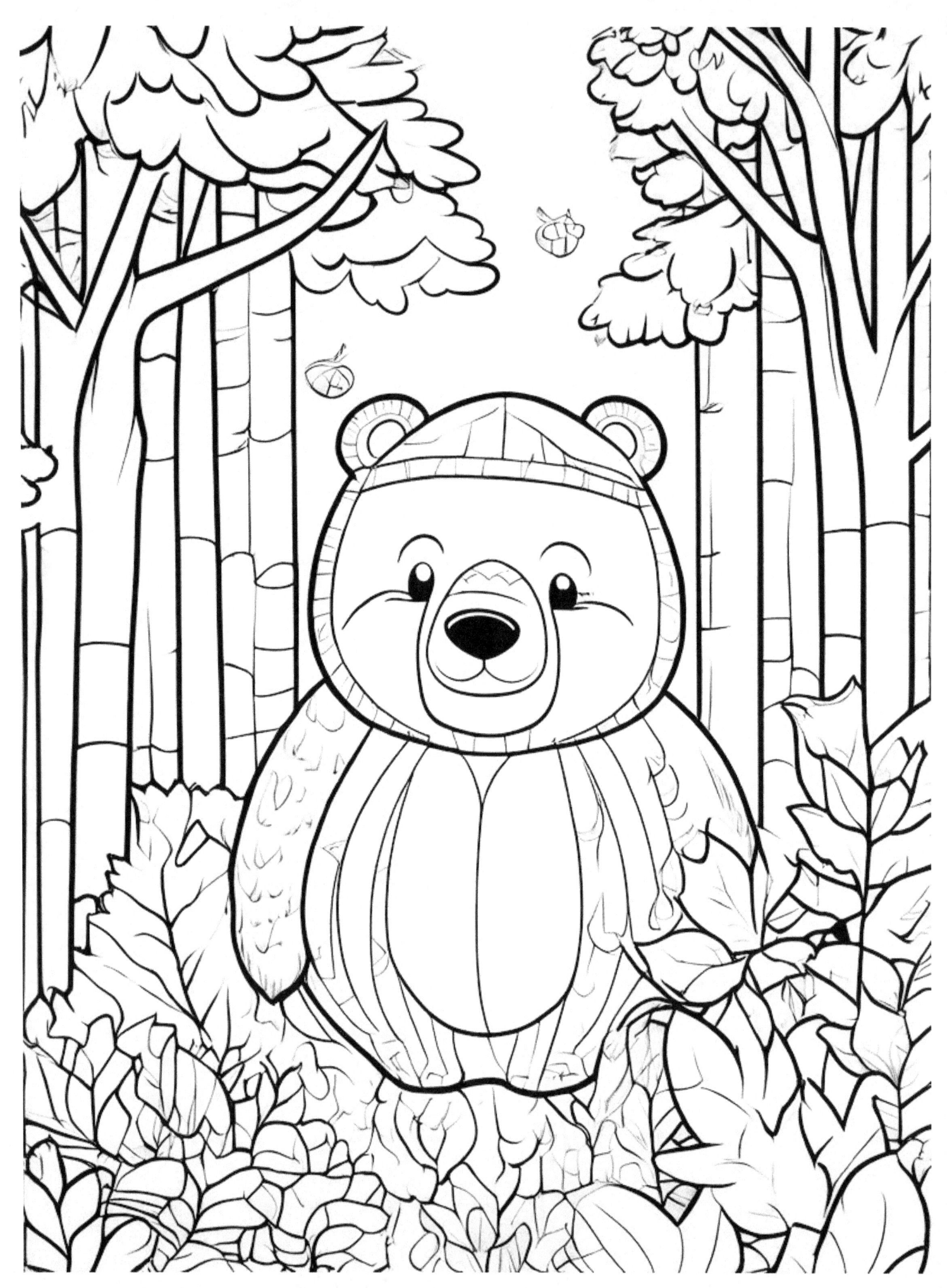

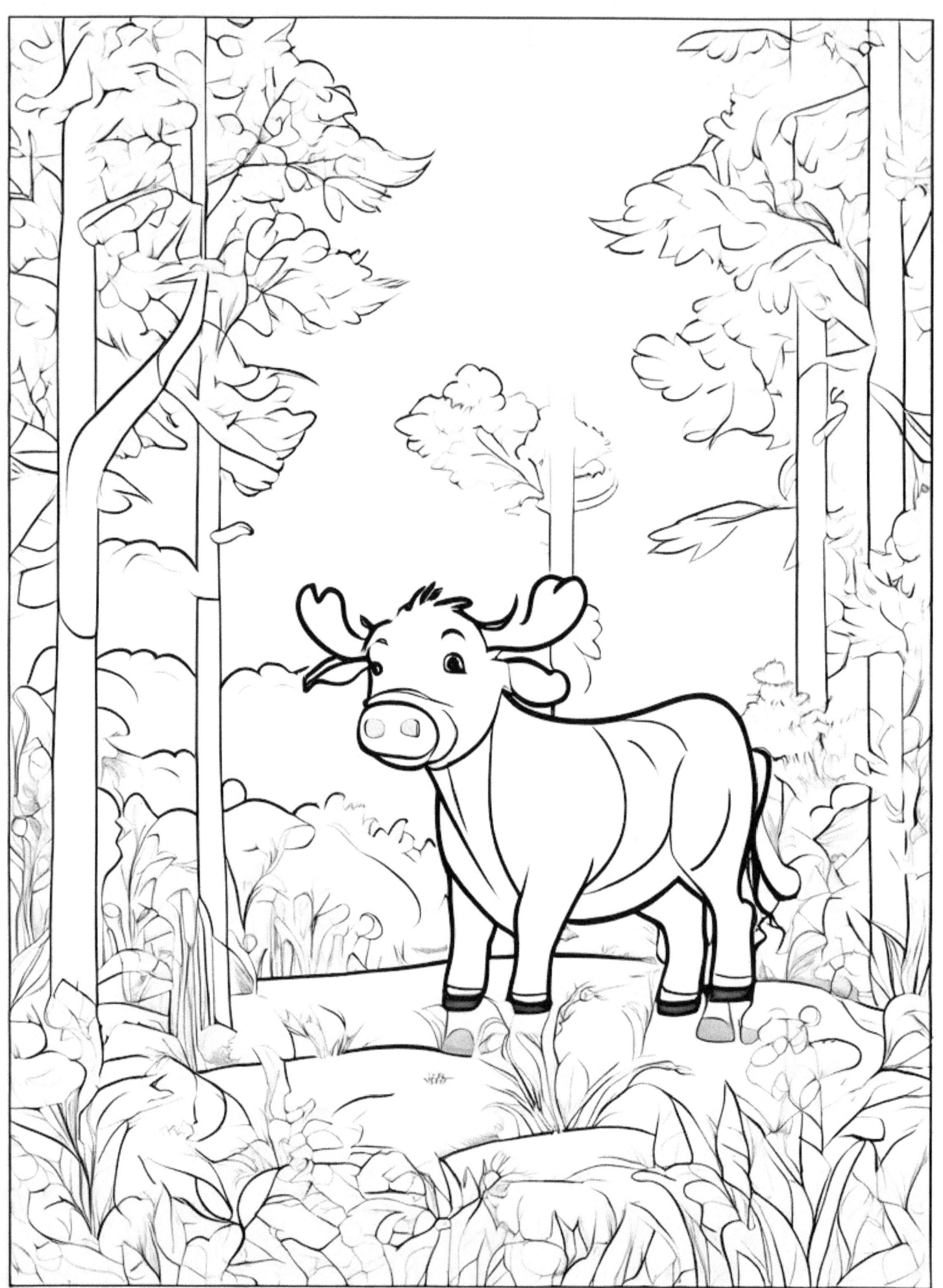

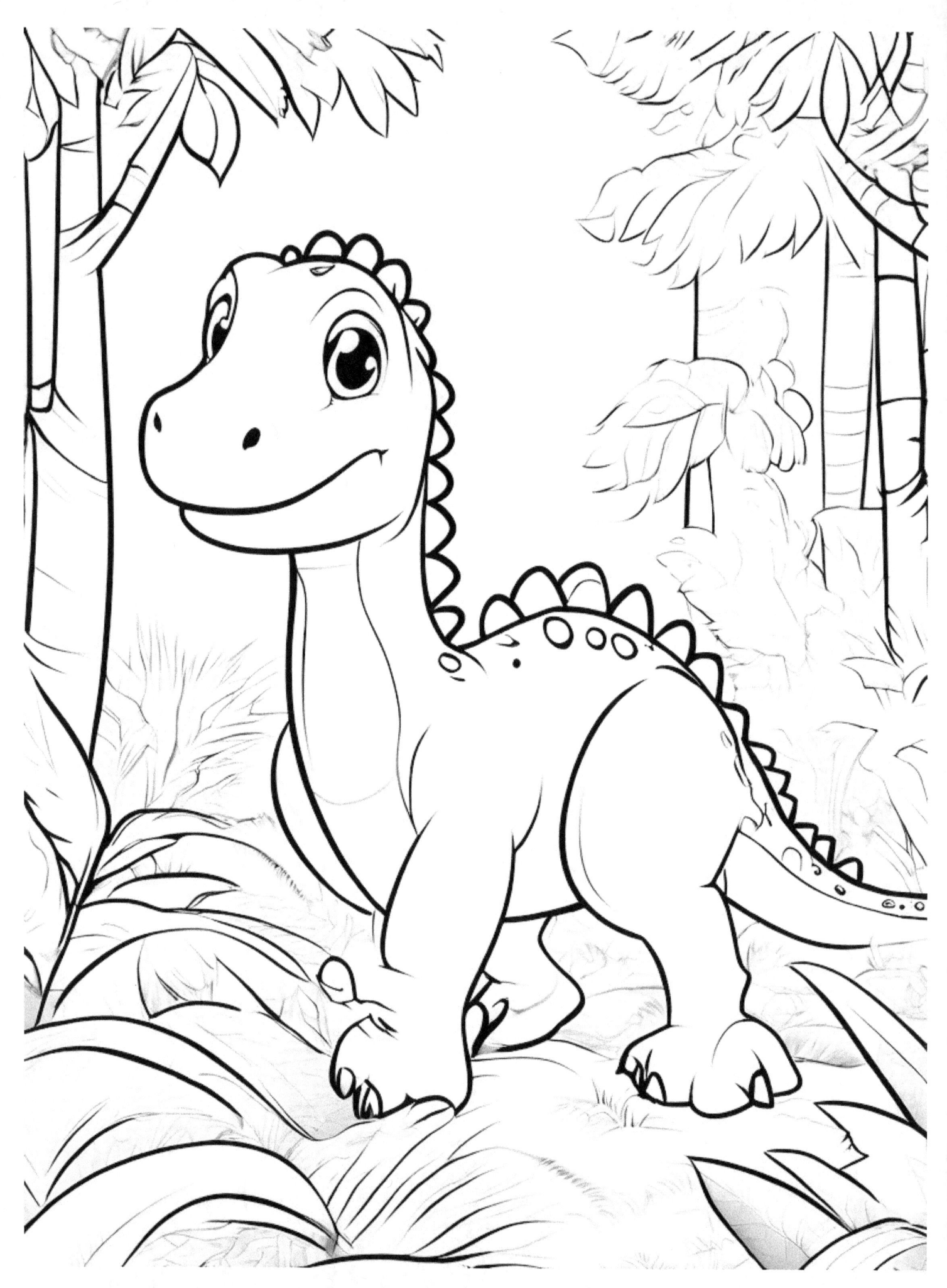

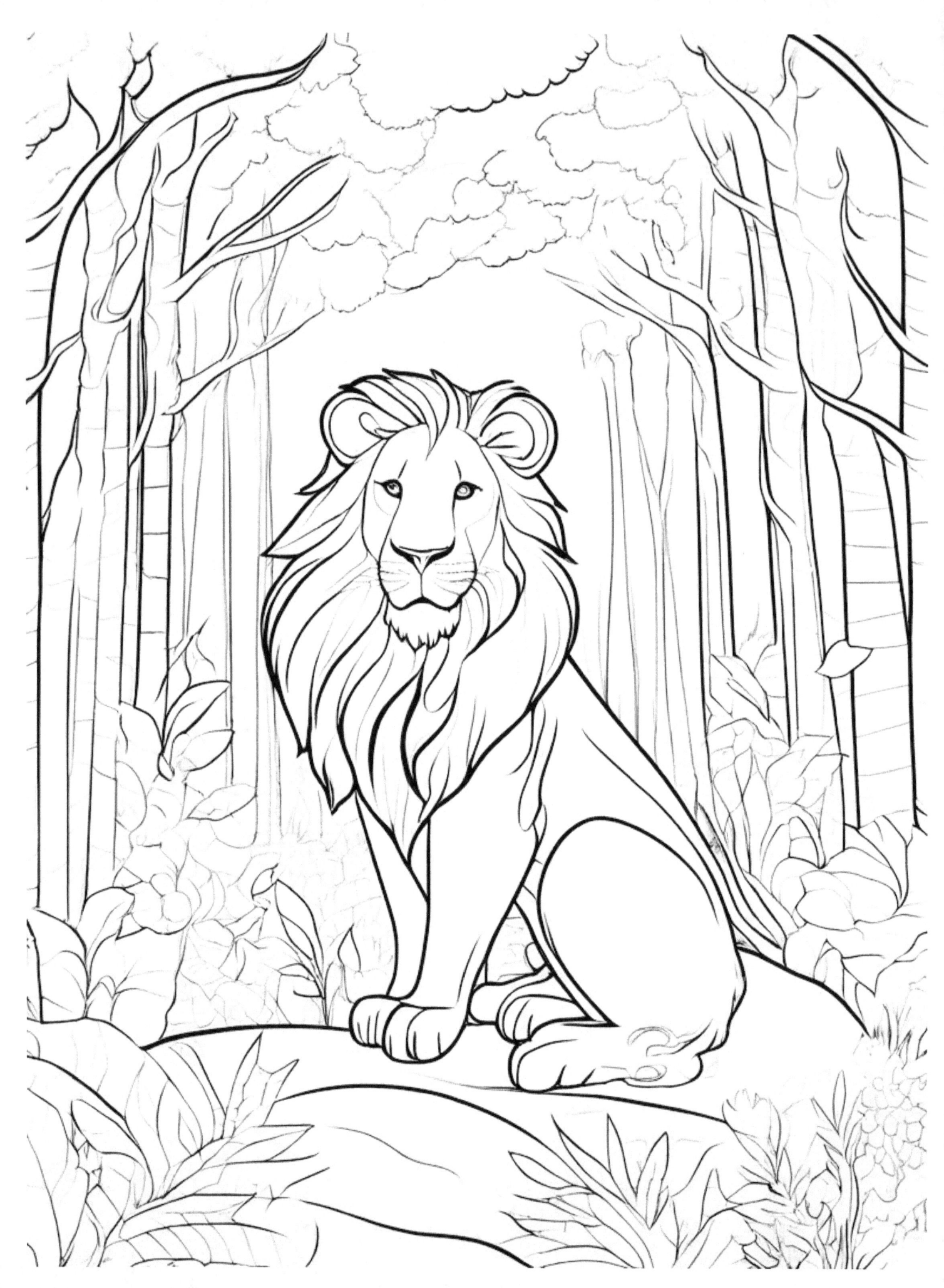

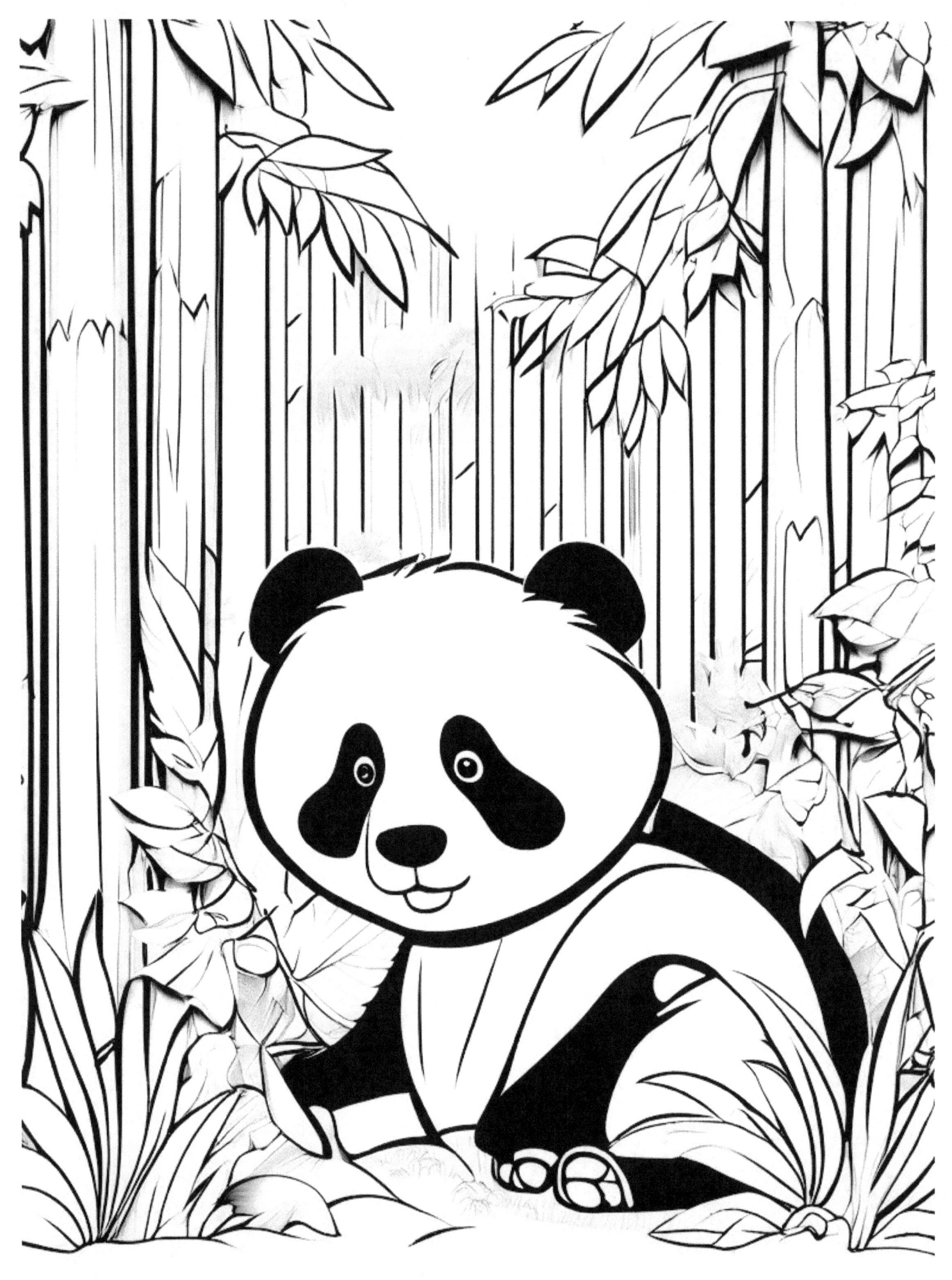

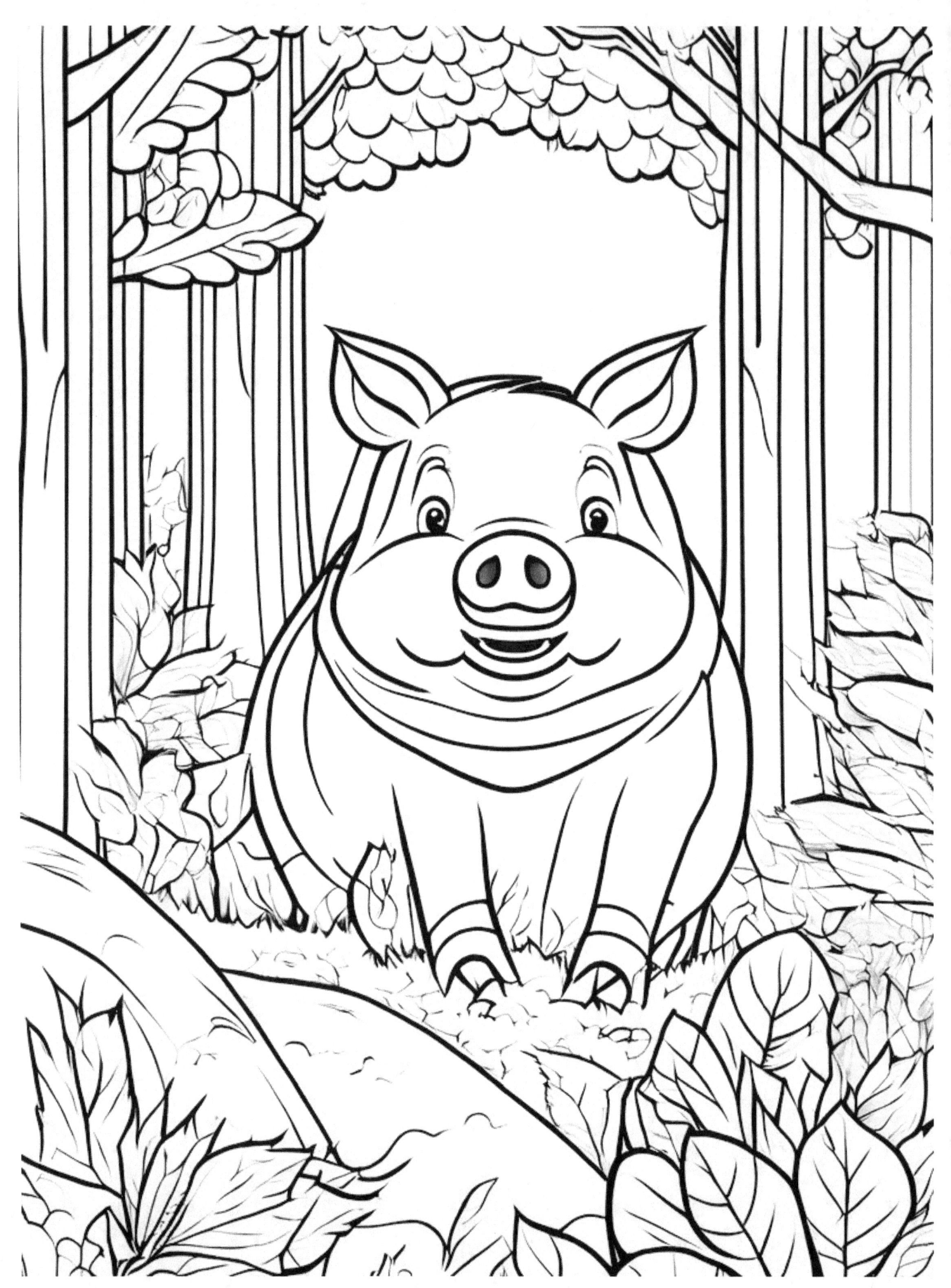

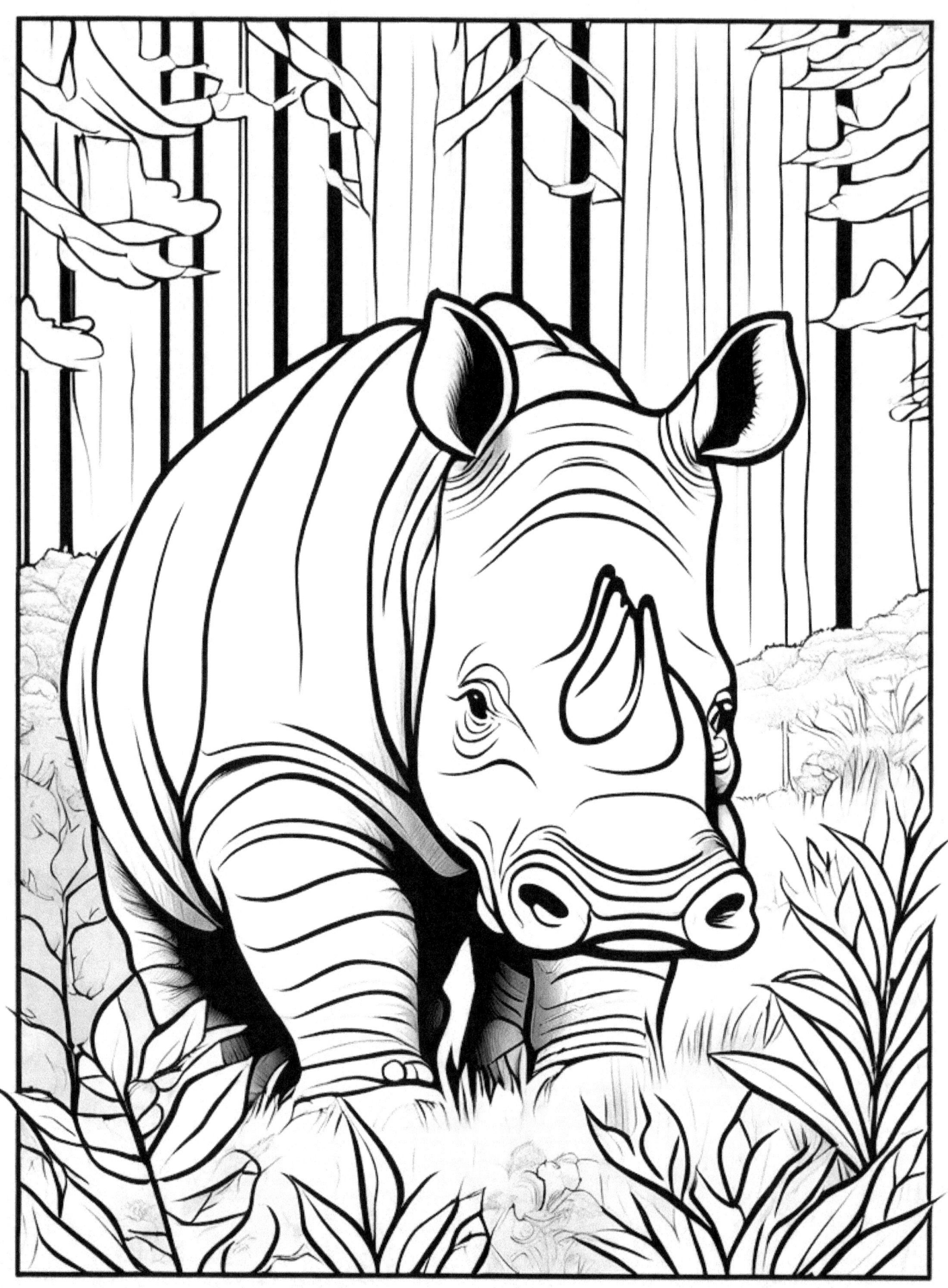

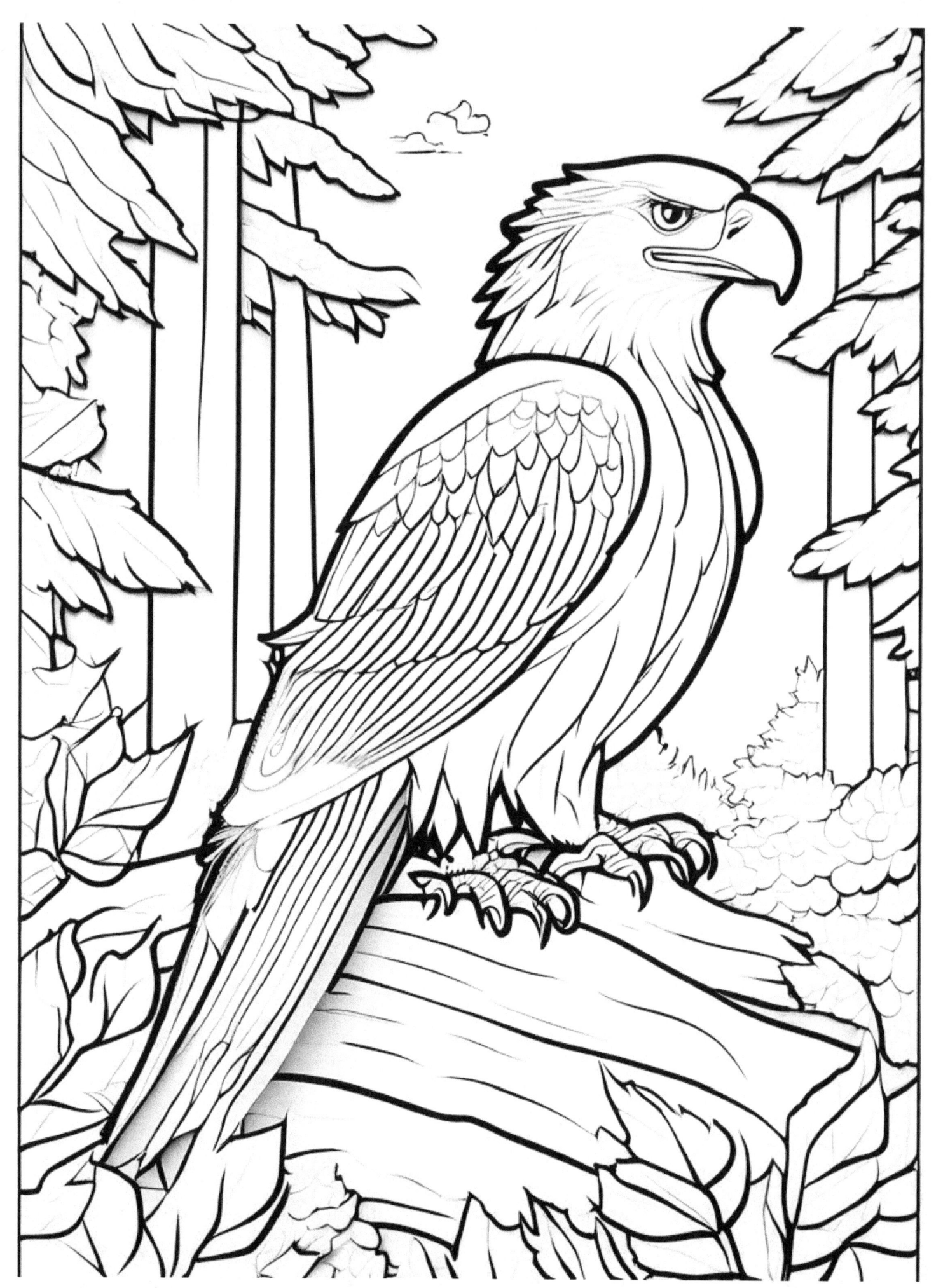

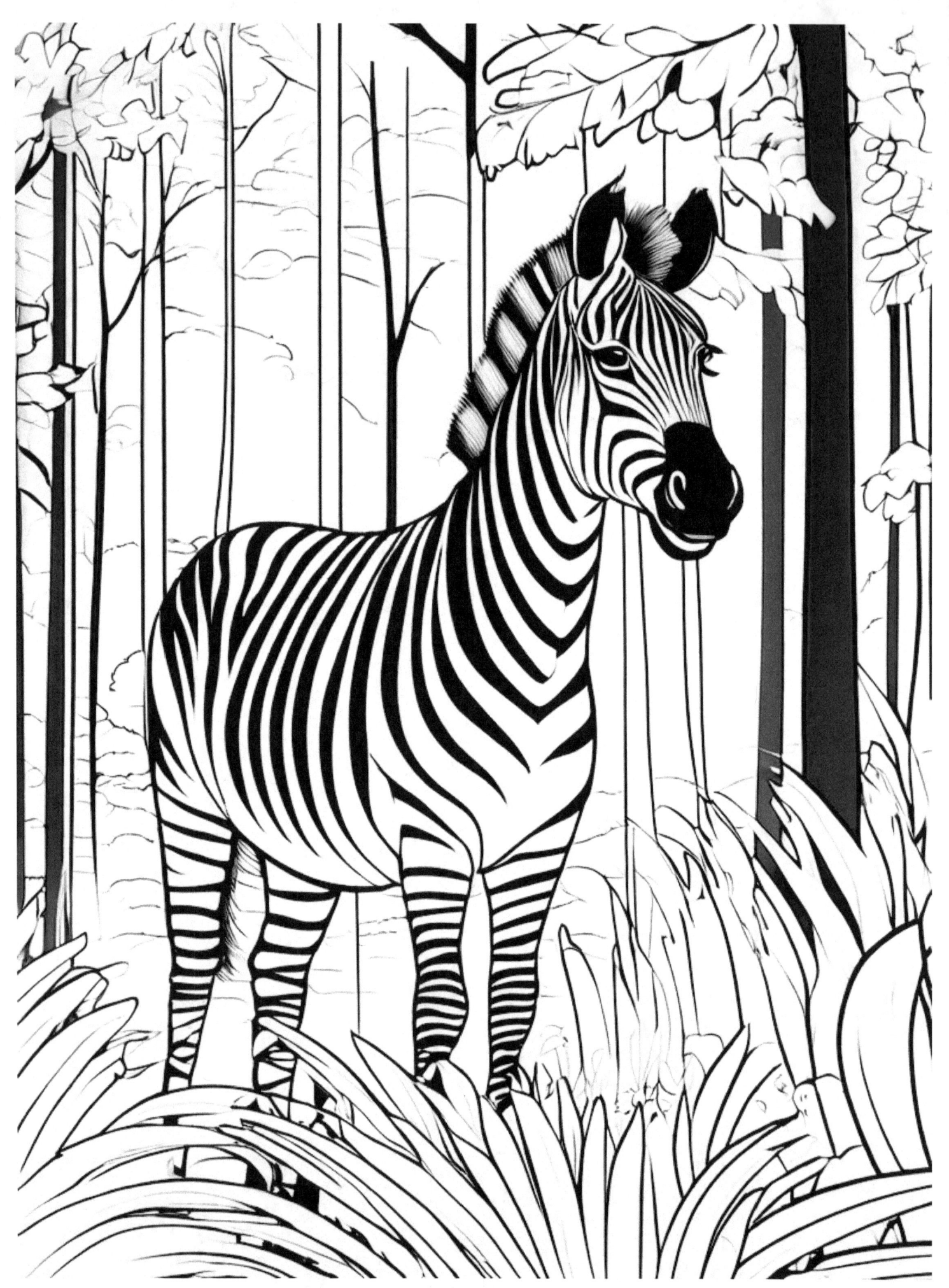

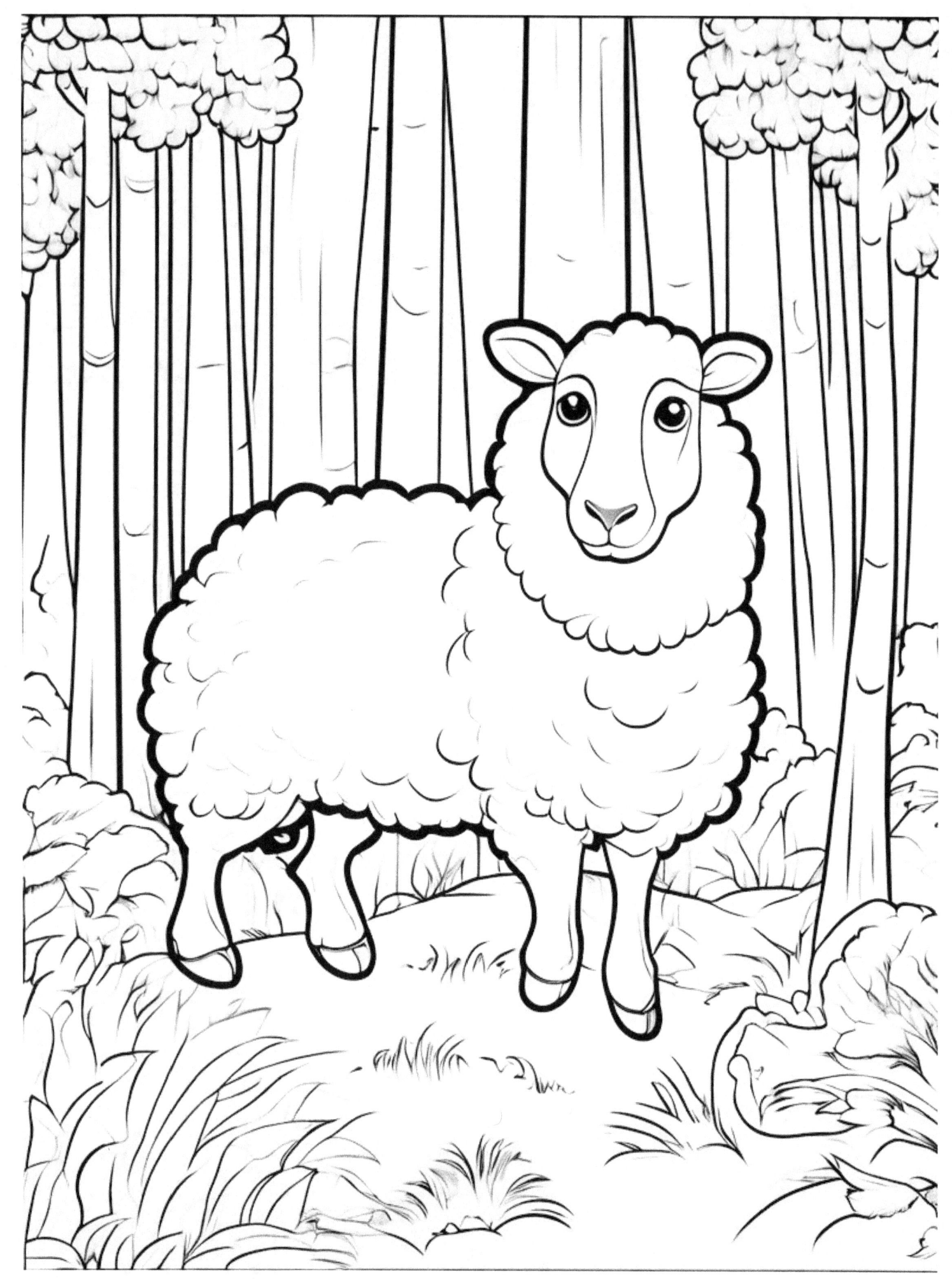

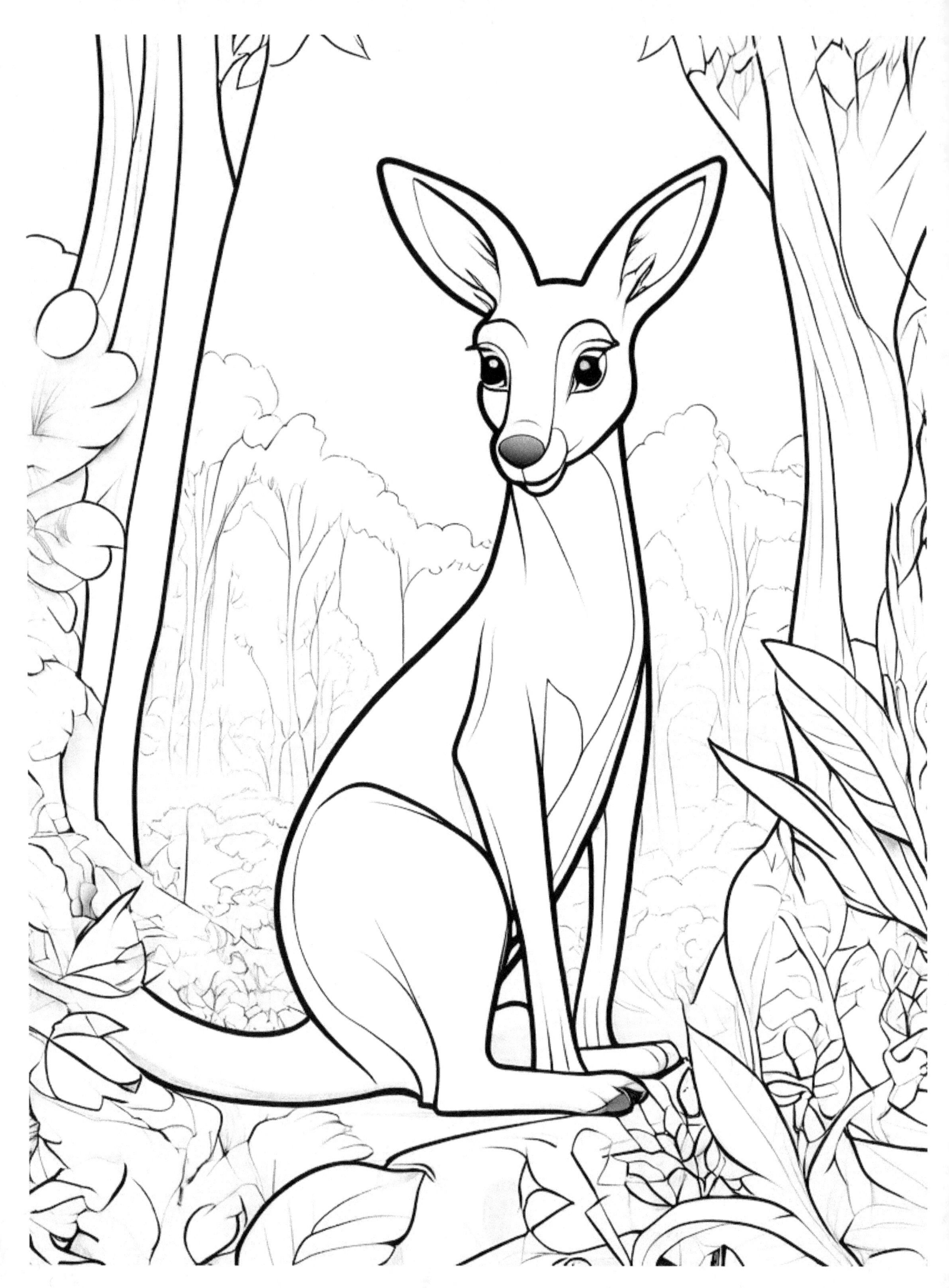

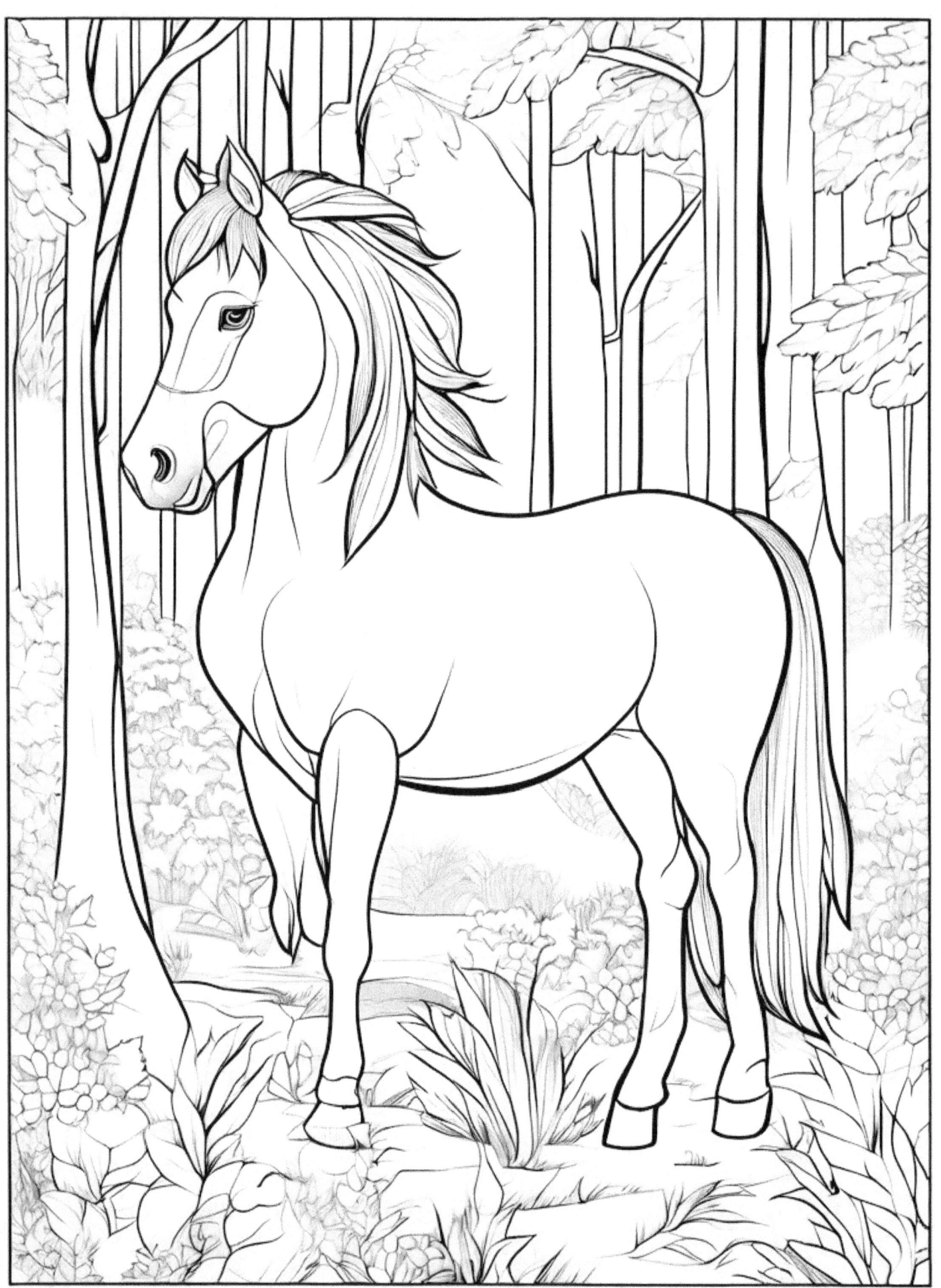

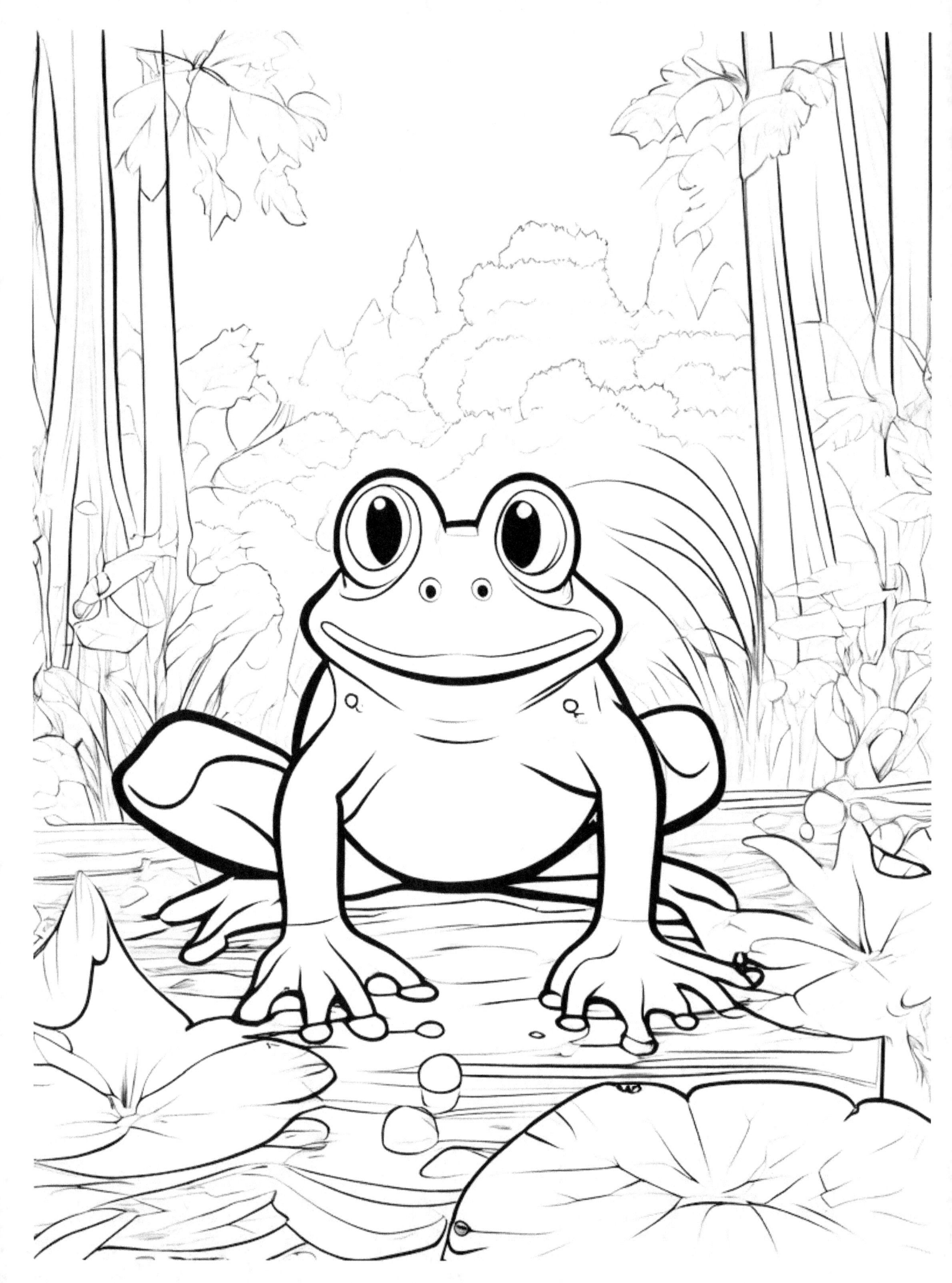

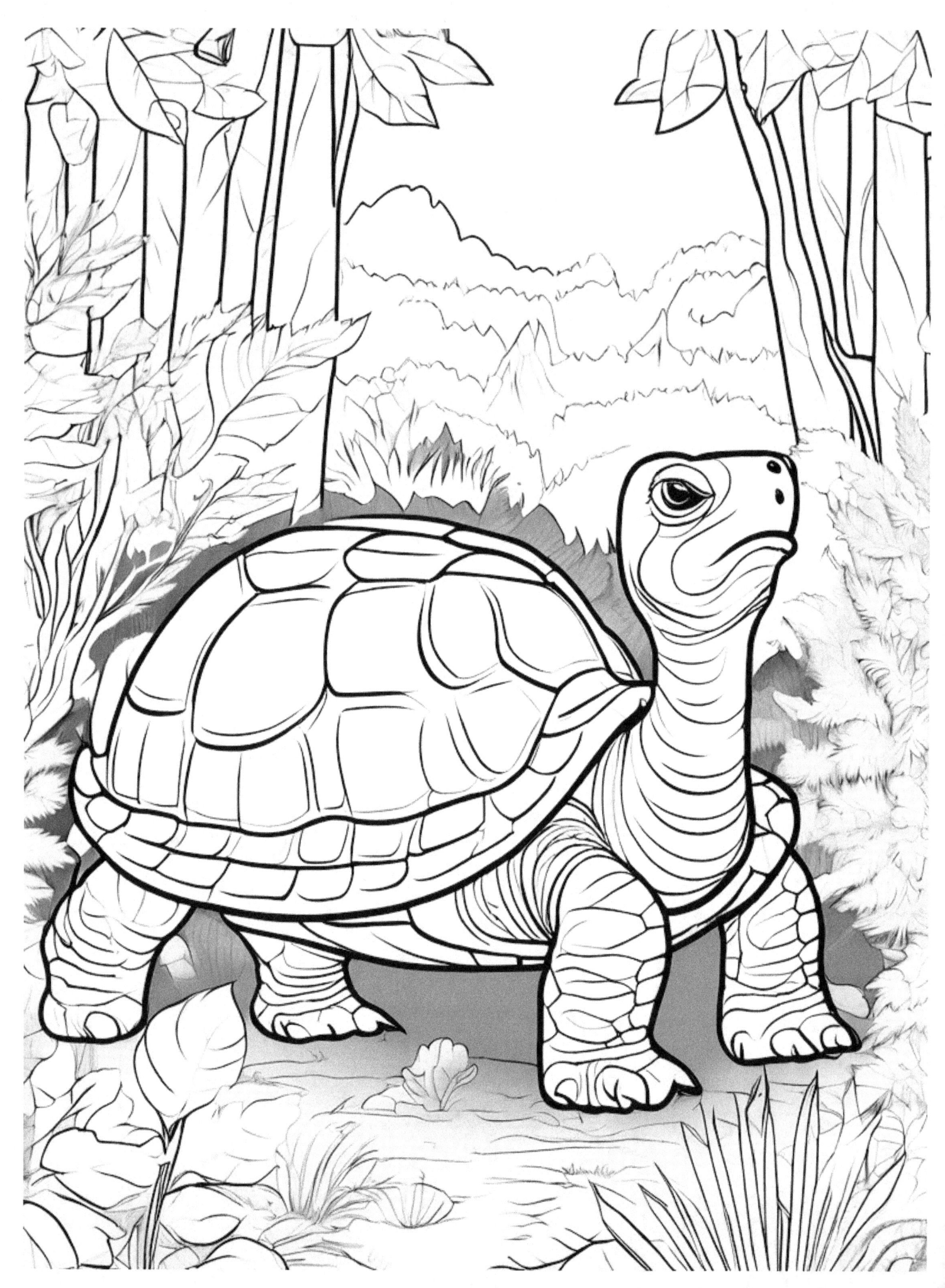

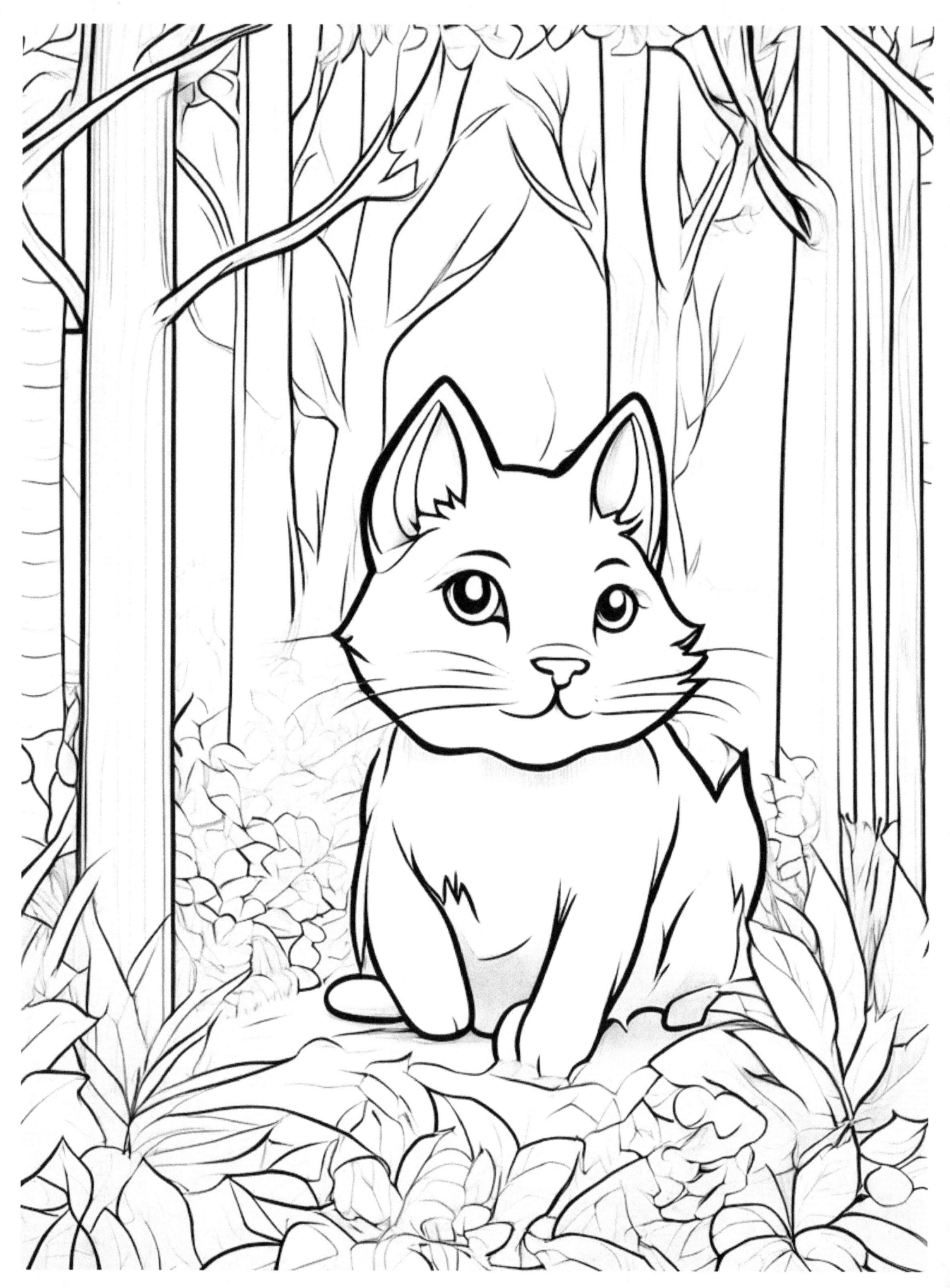

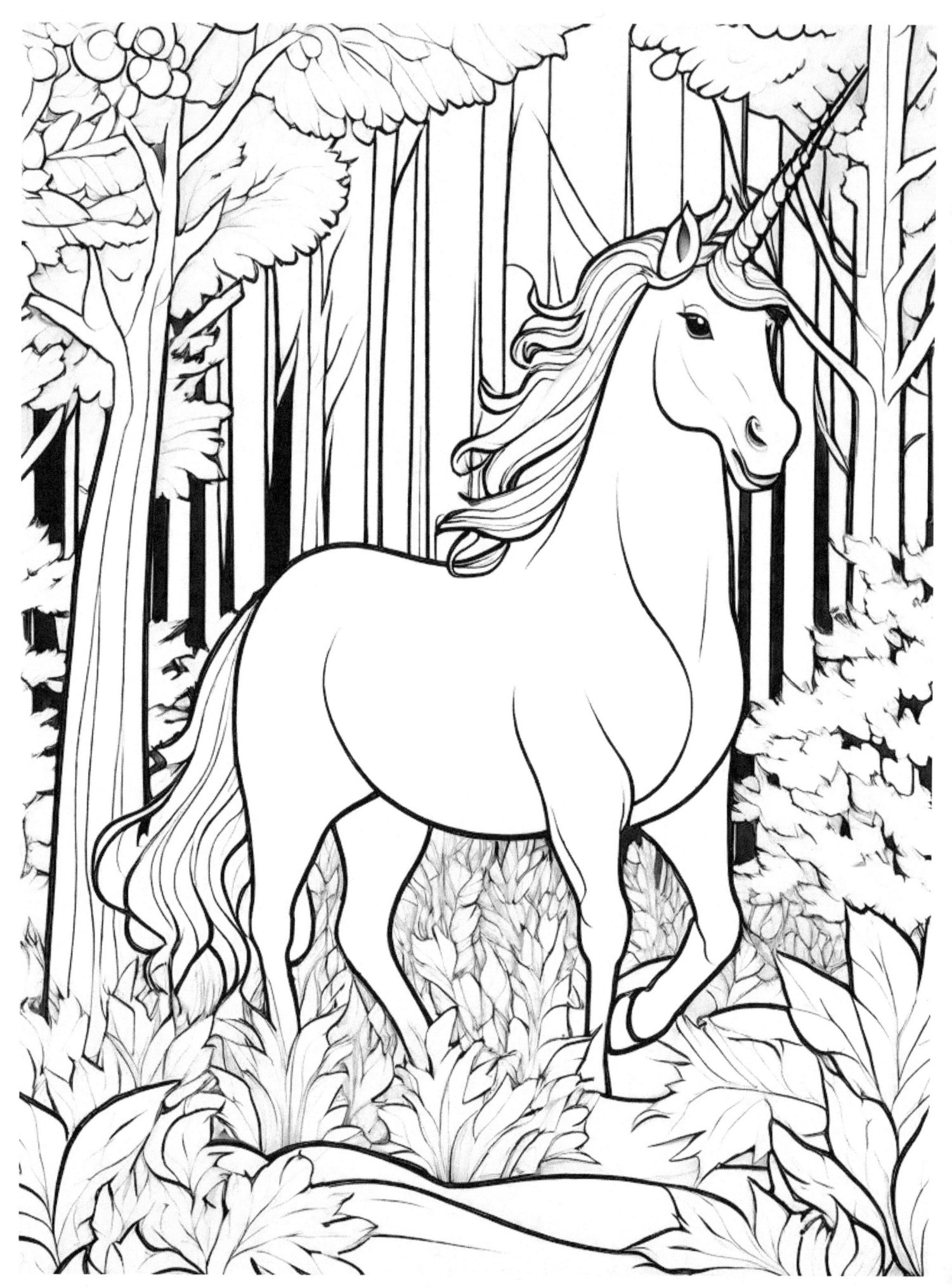

www.ingramcontent.com/pod-product-compliance
Lightning Source LLC
Chambersburg PA
CBHW062119220526
45471CB00010B/3802